WALT DISNEY WORLD HIDDEN HISTORY

Remnants of Former Attractions and Other Tributes

Kevin Yee

Ultimate Orlando Press
Orlando, Florida

Walt Disney World Hidden History: Remnants of Former Attractions and Other Tributes
by Kevin Yee

Published by
ULTIMATE ORLANDO PRESS
www.ultimateorlando.com

All rights reserved. No part of this book may be reproduced or transmitted in any form or by any means, electronic or mechanical, including photocopying, recording or by any information storage and retrieval system without written permission from the author, except for the inclusion of brief quotations in a review.

Cover design by Kevin Yee
Copyright © 2014 Ultimate Orlando Press

This book makes reference to various Disney copyrighted characters, trademarks, marks, and registered marks owned by The Walt Disney Company and Disney Enterprises, Inc.

Walt Disney World Hidden History is not endorsed by, sponsored by, or connected with The Walt Disney Company and/or Disney Enterprises, Inc. in any way.

SECOND EDITION
2014 Printing
Printed in the United States of America

To my family.

No book is written entirely in seclusion. This one came into being with the patient help of numerous sources, readers, and friends, among them **Tony Baxter, Bruce Gordon, Joe Lanzisero, Kim Irvine, Doug Hartwell, Bob Baranick, Eddie Sotto, Bob Gurr, Chris Merritt, Josh Shipley, Bill Watkins, Jim Korkis, Lonnie Hicks, Duncan Dickson, Reed Cunningham, John Frost, Matt Heitzmann, Dan Morrow, Doobie and Rebekah Moseley,** *and* **Jorge Morales.** *My coauthor on the Disneyland books,* **Jason Schultz,** *was invaluable in the early research process for this book as well.*

Numerous bloggers over the years have helped to ferret out tributes and homages as they run across them in the course of their normal work, and I benefitted from their research they publish on public pages. I wish to thank especially **Matt Hochberg, Ricky Brigante, Shawn Slater, Lou Mongello, George Taylor, Brent Dodge, Jeff Heimbuch,** *and* **Jim Hill.** *The official DisneyParks Blog has also been of great use over the years in supplying background about additional tributes.*

A few discoveries can be made simply by walking the parks and looking carefully. Helping me on numerous quests for hidden treasure were **Robert and Ed Bearden, David Jodeit, David Renteria, Paul Lalli, Jeff Lange, Denise Preskitt, Frank Levy,** *and* **Evan Dworkin.**

Enormous thanks go to my proofreaders **Paul Lalli, David Renteria,** *and* **David Jodeit***. They saved me from myself on innumerable occasions.*

Finally, I want to give thanks to my wife and sons for their patience and understanding during the genesis of this book. They enrich my life every day.

Table of Contents

Introduction 9
Magic Kingdom 10
Epcot 56
Disney's Hollywood Studios 76
Disney's Animal Kingdom 107
General Walt Disney World 116
Attraction Dates 122
Main Street Windows 126
Bonus Chapter: History at Universal Studios Florida 128
Afterword 133
About the Author 134
Index 135

Introduction

The constantly-evolving nature of Walt Disney World is part of its allure. Every year the theme parks reinvent and redefine themselves, often by introducing new attractions and replacing older ones. The designers of the attractions, called Imagineers (a term coined by Walt Disney himself to merge both "imagination" and "engineers"), frequently show their reverence for "what came before" by reusing small reminders of former rides in newer ones.

These homages are scattered about like Easter eggs left for visitors to find, and are sometimes accompanied by other tributes: inside jokes about thematic elements, reused figures and characters, even personal touches like the designers' own initials incorporated into thematic elements in the show. These tributes and inside references deposit layers of meaning and history to a form of entertainment often enjoyed on the strengths of its surface value alone. They impart ulterior significance to the attractions and the people who design them, and ultimately remind us why we found them so special in the first place.

The level of attention paid to even the least noticeable details helps impart to Walt Disney World its distinctive magic. Savoring the details will enrich the experience, no matter how often you visit.

Kevin Yee

Magic Kingdom

Wonders of Life Arch
The arch holding the "Magic Kingdom" sign at the parking lot booths for the Transportation and Ticket Center comes from the former Wonders of Life pavilion at Epcot. Before the pavilion was converted to seasonal use and employed as a festival center, it had this arch across its entry way.

Richard Irvine, Joe Potter, and Admiral Joe Fowler
Disney executive Richard Irvine, retired Admiral Joe Fowler, and retired Army General Joe Potter were central figures in the construction of Walt Disney World. Today, the ferries crossing the Seven Seas Lagoon are named after them. On the bottom level of each ferry, a large portrait and a brief biography of that ferry's namesake can be found.

Walt Disney's Window
Walt Disney is honored with a window directly on the train station, high above ground level and facing out toward the Main Entrance of the park. He actually has a second window located at the other end of Main Street, as well.

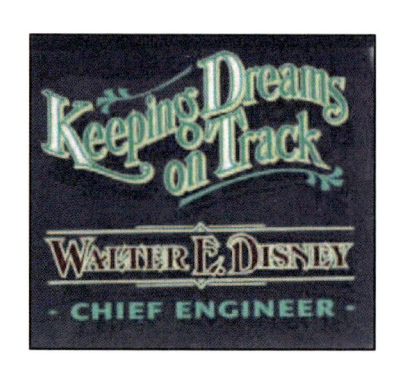

Ticket Book Advertisements

Attraction posters in the tunnels under the train station are holdovers from the days when the Magic Kingdom used ticket books. Before the all-day passport debuted in 1980, patrons had to buy individual ride tickets, and the park therefore had an incentive to advertise lesser-traveled attractions.

Chamber of Commerce

A sign at the entrance to the Chamber of Commerce in Town Square claims it was established in 1871, which is a nod to the opening year of the Magic Kingdom. There are no accidental mentions of "71" in this park, which opened in 1971.

Roy's Bench

A bench in Town Square honors Roy O. Disney, who opened Walt Disney World after his brother passed away in 1966. Walt Disney's role in the company's theme parks is obvious, and his tributes—such as the "Partners" statue with Mickey Mouse in the center of the Magic Kingdom—are equally hard to miss. But his brother Roy Disney was the one who lived to see Walt Disney World opened in 1971. He is honored in today's Magic Kingdom with a statue sitting on a bench in Town Square. The materials and composition of Roy's statue are deliberate echoes of the more visible "Partners" statue of Walt with Mickey, and the statue of Roy posing with Minnie Mouse offers a bookend to Main Street. A photo of Roy from the dedication can also be seen inside City Hall.

Train Photos

Photographs below the Main Street Train Station honor The Walt Disney Company's long history with trains. Some of the pictures adorning the walls of the stroller rental area show the Magic Kingdom's locomotives as they existed in their former industrial lives, and other nearby photographs feature Walt Disney and the miniature backyard train at his Holmby Hills estate.

Imagineer Ward Kimball

A Sorcerers of the Magic Kingdom portal themed to look like an information board gives subtle tribute to Disney employee and fellow train enthusiast Ward Kimball. The board mentions Ward's personal full-sized train, which he dubbed Grizzly Flats, and had kept at his own property. Marceline refers to Walt's original home in Missouri, and Carolwood Park is a tribute to Walt's backyard train that he dubbed the Carolwood Pacific. The other names on the sign honor live-action Disney movies set in idyllic towns similar to Main Street U.S.A. Lem Siddons was a character in the film *Follow Me, Boys*, set in the town of Hickory. Medfield was a college in some movies like *The Absent-Minded Professor* and a town in others, such as the *Shaggy D.A.* Harrington and Pendergast are names from *Pollyanna*. *The Adventures of Bullwhip Griffin* is a movie starring Roddy McDowell. The entire information board, now digital, is itself a kind of tribute, since a physical board with most of the same names occupied a nearby wall until Sorcerers of the Magic Kingdom started in 2012.

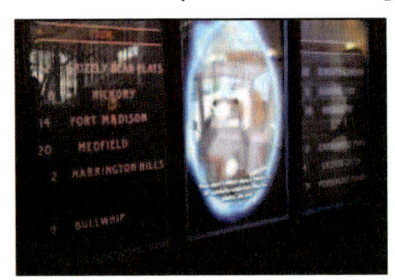

Magic Kingdom's Opening Year

The fire station on Main Street pays tribute to the year that the Magic Kingdom opened. Though above-ground construction started in 1969, the Magic Kingdom did not open until 1971. In honor of that year, the fire station purports to be "Engine Co. 71" in brass lettering visible high on the building's front side. Inside the station, a barrel makes another mention of Engine Company 71. A sign halfway up Main Street at one doorway near the Athletic Club also mentions that the "casting agency" has been open since '71. This doorway sign pays tribute to the Cast Members at Walt Disney World throughout the years.

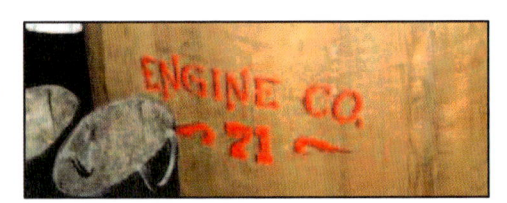

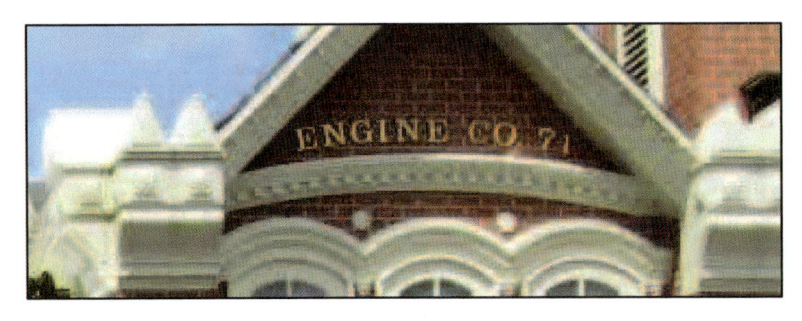

Original Dapper Dans

A drawing on the wall of the Harmony Barber Shop shows the likeness of the original four Dapper Dans, the barbershop quartet which roams Main Street entertaining visitors. Since they got their start inside the barber shop, it seemed a logical place for a tribute.

Turn-of-the-Century America

Up the road, a sign above one doorway for the Emporium "expansion" claims this building dates back to 1901—the year Walt Disney was born. A colorful mural near the ceiling just inside this section of the Emporium also mentions 1901. Main Street purports to be a sanitized version of a typical small American town circa 1890-1910, a period during which Walt was heavily influenced by his time spent as a child in the small town of Marceline, Missouri. Traces of this time frame are everywhere. For instance, gas lamps exist side by side with electric lights along the street, capturing the moment when America "went electric." Antique mutoscopes, which approximate a film by flipping through static pictures, entertain visitors at the Main Street train station. They were moved to the train station when the Penny Arcade was converted to a shop, while other mutoscopes moved to the Boardwalk resort and the prop warehouse at Disney's Hollywood Studio's Backlot Tour.

Window Homages

Many of the windows along the second story of Main Street are decorated with the names of important individuals who made significant contributions to Walt Disney World. From General Joe Potter, the construction expert who oversaw the building of the Magic Kingdom, to Earl Vilmer, who renovated the Walt Disney World Railroad locomotives, these windows give credit to the often overlooked people whose years of hard work enabled the Magic Kingdom to thrive. At Disneyland, where the tradition of using such second-story windows to honor important company officials began, a majority of the people honored are artists and engineers (dubbed "Imagineers") who helped build and design that park. At the Magic Kingdom, there are more managers and administrators listed, such as the onetime head of Walt Disney World security, the chief Walt Disney World accountant, or the director of the Walt Disney World paint shop. Roy E. Disney's window references his sailboat, the *Peregrina*.

Chicago World's Fair

Thomas McCrumb, at one time listed as the proprietor of the candy store on Main Street via stenciled letters on a window, was actually the personal dentist to a young Walt Disney (he once commissioned one of Walt's earliest films, called *Tommy Tucker's Tooth*). The backstory of this store is that McCrumb visited the 1893 Chicago World's Columbian Exposition (look for a poster of a woman on the wall by the cashier to this effect, and a model of a complicated contraption on a nearby shelf), where he was so impressed by the gears and levers of machination that he added such automation to his own candy shop back on Main Street. There's even a further connection to that same world's fair: parts of it were built by Walt Disney's father Elias when he worked as a contractor. Unsurprisingly, elsewhere on Main Street, Elias Disney has his own window, where he is listed as a contractor. The same 1893 Chicago World's Fair is also referenced in the Crystal Arts store—look for a glass red chalice atop one display case with telltale lettering.

Walt's Birth Year

The date 1901 is emblazoned across the tile floor of the Town Square Theater in honor of Walt Disney's year of birth. This facility was originally home to Exposition Hall and included two screening theaters used in later years to show old Disney cartoons. It closed in 2011 to make room for Disney's Storybook Princesses and Backstage Magic with Mickey Mouse. The year is also mentioned in one hallway painting of Exposition Hall.

Animators Wilfred Jackson, Fred Moore, and Ward Kimball

The artist behind some of the earliest Disney company successes, the Silly Symphonies, is honored on a painting in the queue for Backstage Magic with Mickey Mouse. On a painting of a gondola scene, an ad in the upper-right mentions "Wilfred Jaxson" [Jackson], and a nearby ad for "Walter D." leaves little to the imagination either! The scene depicted comes from a vintage cartoon called *The Nifty Nineties*, which highlighted a vaudeville act called *The Two Men From Illinois*—the characters shown were clear caricatures of animators Fred Moore and Ward Kimball. To bring the reference full circle, a sign on a corkboard at the queue of the attraction mentions that Mickey's opening act will be "Fred and Ward."

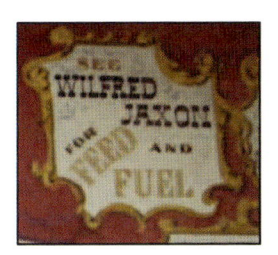

Marketing Executive Scott Tilley

Real-life Disney marketing executive Scott Tilley is honored in the post office room in the queue of Backstage Magic with Mickey Mouse. The corkboard on the wall includes a letter from the "Art and Publicity Dept" of the theater and comes from S.A. Tilley.

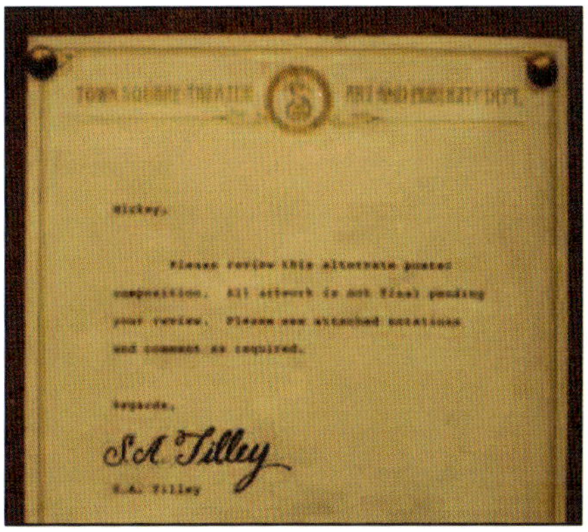

Animator Bill Justice

Legendary Disney artist Bill Justice is given a place of honor in the mail room section of the queue for Backstage Magic with Mickey Mouse. Justice created an enormous mural of dozens of Disney characters for the Town Square Theater when it was new, and for many years this was a source of wonder for visitors leaving the cinema area. While the character mural was removed for the renovation of the space for Magician Mickey Mouse, a reminder exists in the mail room. Not only is there a mail slot for "B. Justice," if you peek carefully at what's in that slot, you'll find a small version of that famous mural, rolled up to fit into the slot!

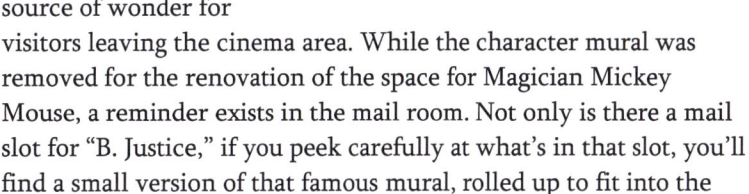

Journey Into Imagination Lyrics

The poster in the meeting room for Backstage Magic with Mickey Mouse pays tribute to an original EPCOT Center attraction. The poster of a Tesla coil includes the phrase "magic that lights up the stage and sparks your imagination," a reference to Journey into Imagination, where similar lyrics were used in the theme song of that Future World attraction. On the same poster, look to the top to see the familiar star-and-moon-sliver from Mickey's Sorcerer hat that is used as a corporate logo for Walt Disney Imagineering.

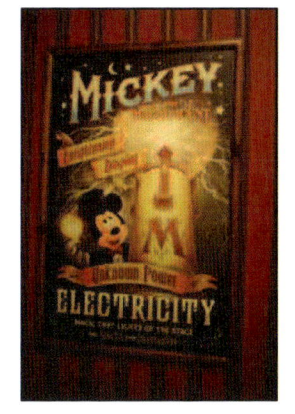

Disney Attractions Locations

The traveling trunks visible at the start of Backstage Magic with Mickey Mouse are decorated with stickers showing where they have previously traveled, and the list of places visited reads like a Disney travelogue, including such locales as the Disney Cruise Line private island Castaway Cay, Hong Kong (where there is a Disneyland), the Grand Floridian Resort, Paris (where there are two Disney parks), the secret members-only Club 33 in Disneyland, Colonel Haithi (who is an elephant in the *Jungle Book*, but also gives his name to a restaurant at Disneyland Paris), and the Mira Costa hotel at Tokyo Disneyland.

Hidden Oswald

A drawing of Oswald the Lucky Rabbit, the predecessor to Mickey Mouse as the Disney company's main cartoon character, can be seen in a hand-drawn image on the corkboard in Backstage Magic with Mickey Mouse. Oswald had been purchased by a competing studio early in Disney's history, and Walt created Mickey Mouse in response. Decades later, in 2006, the Walt Disney Company reacquired the rights to the character. This drawing was made by Imagineer Jason Grandt while still a child, and was reproduced here as his own inside joke.

Mr. Toad's Wild Ride

A letter on the desk in Backstage Magic with Mickey Mouse is a unique item in that it is neither a normal tribute nor a plain remnant, but rather a tribute to a remnant! Before Mickey Mouse moved into this space, the Exposition Hall was home to a remnant from a long-closed attraction, Mr. Toad's Wild Ride, in the form of one ride vehicle. When Mickey moved in, this letter (on Toad Hall stationary and signed by Angus McBadger) thanks M. Mouse for purchasing their horseless carriage from the "Nifty Nineties," a reference to the car's time here during the 1990s.

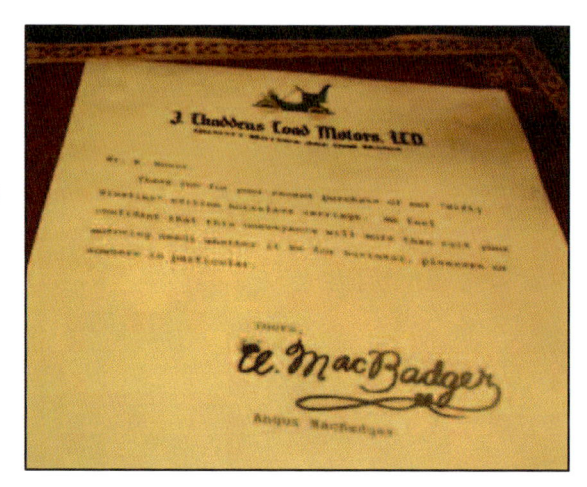

Mary Poppins

There are references to *Mary Poppins* scattered throughout Backstage Magic with Mickey Mouse, such as the "talking" parrot head for the umbrella, and a birdseed bag carrying the name "Tuppence"—a reference to the song "Feed the Birds" from the movie. The flipped-open trunk with the umbrella also features items from the two wizards in *Sword and the Stone*, another Disney animated feature, and watch for other references to Mickey Mouse cartoons (such as "The Band Concert") throughout the room.

WED Illusioneering

A sub-department of the better-known Walt Disney Imagineering (which is short for "imagination engineering"), Illusioneering refers to the art of designing illusions for use in the theme parks, such as the tricks of the eye in the Haunted Mansion or the Magic Mirror in Enchanted Tales with Belle. A nod to this department comes in the form of the blueprint in one corner of Backstage Magic with Mickey Mouse, which is said to be created by WED Illusioneering—a fitting tribute, since the blueprint is for an illusion called the Saw of Dread!

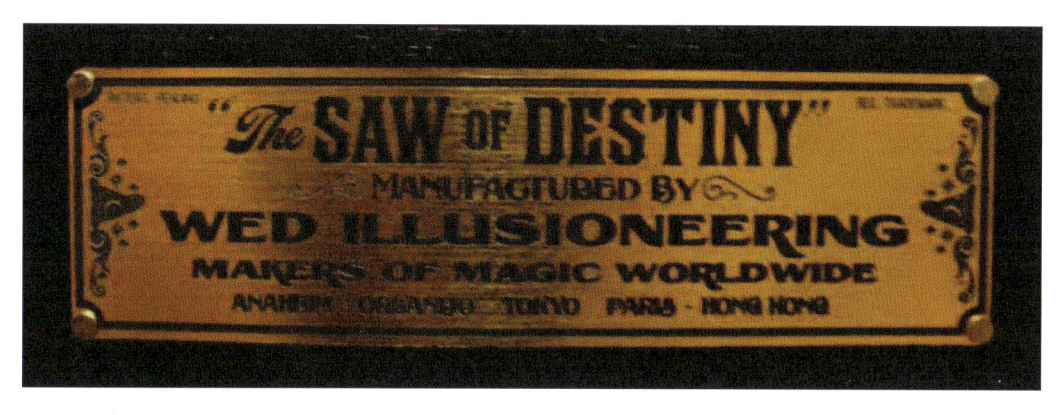

Imagineer Joyce Carlson

The bird cooing in the birdcage at Backstage with Mickey Mouse reproduces the "disappearing butterfly" trick you may have seen at Epcot's Imagination ride, but its name – Joyce – is yet another tribute, this time to Imagineer Joyce Carlson, who helped make quite a few of the rides in the Magic Kingdom.

Park Icons

The iconic symbols for each of the four Walt Disney World parks are to be found as tributes in Backstage Magic with Mickey Mouse, high atop a bookshelf. The crystal ball represents Spaceship Earth, the tree is a proxy for the Tree of Life, the sorcerer's hat stands in for Disney's Hollywood Studios, and the collection of books (some with spire designs on the spines) is an abstract version of the castle at the Magic Kingdom.

Madame Leota

The crystal ball in Backstage Magic with Mickey Mouse doubles as a second tribute in the form of the famous Haunted Mansion séance ball, since this crystal ball is labeled "Leota Crystals" as the manufacturer, and is dated 1969—the opening year of the Haunted Mansion in Disneyland.

Mickey's (Bird)House

The shop at the exit to Backstage Magic with Mickey Mouse, Curtain Call Collectibles, includes a remnant from Mickey's Toontown Fair. The main attraction of that former land was Mickey's Country House, which included a barn and an attached garage. In the garage was a birdhouse Mickey was working on, and that birdhouse can now be seen near the ceiling in Curtain Call Collectibles.

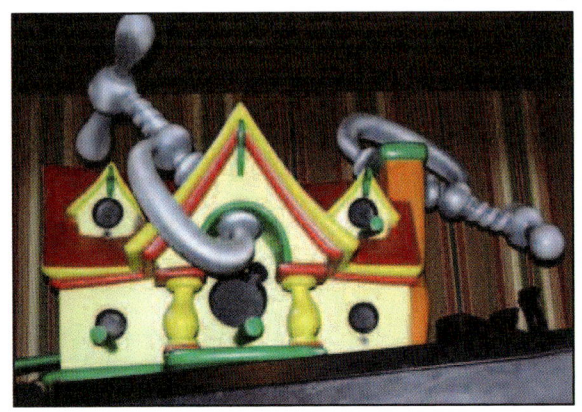

Summer Magic

A 1963 movie called *Summer Magic* provided several songs for the background music heard on Main Street, but even more subtle tributes are found in the character names from the movie. Nancy and Julia, cousins in the film, are listed as the owners of Le Chapeau, and prints of them can be seen in the hallway of Le Chapeau. Osh Popham, the general store owner in the movie, similarly runs the Emporium at Magic Kingdom. His name is stenciled on display windows facing Town Square diagonally.

Walt's Hatbox

The number 63 is visible on the sign for Le Chapeau to reinforce the year of the release of the movie *Summer Magic*. That sign, a hatbox, is also a tribute of a different kind. It reproduces the one from the *Lady and the Tramp* movie, since the nearby Tony's restaurant is themed to that film. In the movie, the husband brings home a puppy in a hatbox, and that hatbox is reproduced here on Main Street. The gag with the puppy in a hatbox originally began life as something Walt himself did for his own wife. The date from *Summer Magic* shows up a second time, as the Emporium is listed as having started operation in 1863 as well.

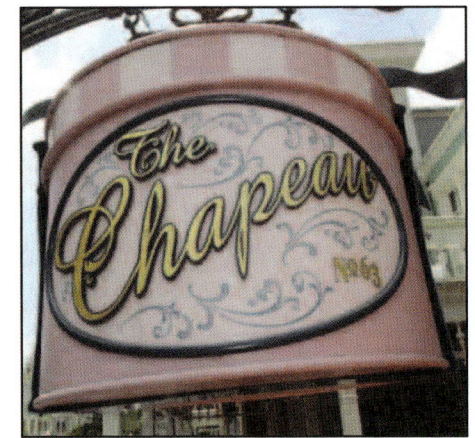

Emporium Imagineers

One painted mural near the ceiling in the Emporium depicts the Imagineers who worked on the expansion of this shop, including Art Director Agnes David-Hoffman, Jim Heffron, Cicero Greathouse, and Katie Roser. Imagineer Joyce Carlson is also here, wearing the flowered hat in the bottom-left, though she did not work on the expansion of the Emporium.

Main Street Cinema

The ceiling of the Main Street Cinema contains a hexagonal box that once housed projectors. This store was once an actual cinema, showing several early Disney cartoons simultaneously on different screens on a looping basis. Multiple screens around the room were employed, and the projector box in the ceiling and boarded up projector windows still show evidence of where the projectors aimed. One of the projectors and one screen were preserved and kept in use when the cinema was replaced by the store in 1998. Because these cartoons had played in the park for so long, park managers wanted to continue to show them to the public, and one of the two Walt Disney Story theaters in Exposition Hall was refurbished for this purpose. Originally the cartoons were silent films, in keeping with the Main Street theme of a turn-of-the-century town. Synchronized sound hadn't been invented yet, nor had Mickey Mouse. Because the public kept asking for Mickey Mouse cartoons, several Mickey shorts were introduced in 1978, which is the year Mickey celebrated his 50th birthday.

Tobacconist Shop

The wooden Indian statue now in front of the Crystal Arts store is a remnant of a tobacconist shop that once sold tobacco products on Main Street. Originally, the statue served as an advertisement for the tobacco shop, when it was located across the street (near today's Hall of Champions). When the tobacco shop closed in 2000, the statue moved across the street to the Market House, which still sold cigarettes. Crystal Arts then expanded in 2006 to take over the Market House, and the Indian now sits as a reminder of what was once available. A duplicate statue can be found in Frontierland, where the thematic link to a general store is even stronger.

Market House

Items atop a display case in Crystal Arts are remnants of the former store in this space. The Crystal Arts store was originally a smaller shop. The space on the "corner" of Center Street was then not Crystal Arts, but the Market House, a representation of the general goods store common at the turn of the century. When Crystal Arts expanded here in 2006, the antique stove and most props were removed, but a few persisted atop display cases, like an antique typewriter and metal scales.

Imagineer Orlando Ferrante

A Disney Imagineer with experience at the seminal 1964-65 World's Fair, Anaheim's Tiki Room, and most of the international Disney parks is honored in tiny font as the proprietor of Crystal Arts. After working on the World's Fair attractions, Ferrante became head of various parts of manufacturing, production, and engineering for all of Walt Disney Imagineering. A framed ceremonial "first dollar" for the Crystal Arts store on one wall also shows the naturalization certificate for one "Tomas Ferrante" and lists his address as "14 Center Street"—exactly where this is located in the Magic Kingdom.

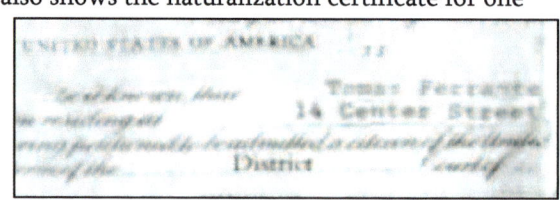

Shell Companies

Windows above the Crystal Arts store on Main Street list the names of the fake ("shell") companies used to buy the land Walt Disney World would be built upon. The forty-three square miles eventually purchased for Walt Disney World had to be bought from multiple owners who would have raised their asking price if they knew Disney was behind the acquisitions, so Walt used secrecy to hide his intentions. To make the purchases, he sent unknown emissaries that ostensibly operated for companies which turned out to not actually exist, including one "Ayefour Corporation" (a subtle reference to the nearby I-4 interstate freeway).

Walt's Window

Walt Disney is honored on a window above the Plaza Ice Cream Parlor. Both Roy O. Disney and his son, Roy E. Disney, have windows on Main Street that acknowledge their lasting influence on the company. At Disneyland, Walt Disney didn't want a window dedicated to himself, but when he died, park designers sought to honor him in this fashion at Walt Disney World. Walt's window is one of the few such tribute windows that face Cinderella Castle, marking the location as a place of honor. This is actually Walt's second window on Main Street. He has another highly visible window at the railroad station, facing out toward the park's main entrance. These two windows make it possible to consider all of Main Street to be like the opening reel of a motion picture which shows the production credits. If the windows on the buildings all along the street give credit to those "behind the camera" making the park come true, Walt's name appropriately comes both first and last, as he is the director of the entire production. It is no coincidence that most of the early Imagineers were artists from movie studios, familiar primarily with storytelling and movie-style showmanship. For this reason, Walt and his artists constructed visual "weenies" to lure visitors to the next "reel" of the "motion picture," such as a castle for Fantasyland or a tall white steamship for Frontierland.

Casey's Corner Imagineers

One team photo on the wall of Casey's Corner is modern, and shows the Imagineers responsible for this restaurant's 1995 refurbishment… including some women, also shown wearing mustaches in the picture!

Plaza Swan Boats

The moat surrounding the Central Plaza was once used for a boat ride in the park's first few years. The Plaza Swan Boats circled the Central Plaza in the Magic Kingdom's early years, gliding around the castle and its carefully manicured lawns, and making a loop around the Swiss Family Treehouse. More of a relaxing atmosphere ride than a mode of transportation, the Swan Boats unfortunately suffered from low capacity and succumbed to the march of time after about ten years. Until 2014, the abandoned dock for the Swan Boats remained amid the rose garden. The front of the Swan Boats were shaped like giant white swans—a thematic nod to Disneyland's longstanding tradition of housing real swans in the moat around its castle.

The Best Time of Your Life

A song heard in the background musical loop at Tomorrowland Terrace is an instrumental version of a now-defunct song from Carousel of Progress. From 1975-1993, the theme song of the attraction (which had undergone many changes and updates over the years) was "The Best Time of Your Life" rather than the original song "There's a Great Big Beautiful Tomorrow" (which returned to the attraction in 1993).

Walt's Future City

The model visible from the PeopleMover ride was created as the original vision of EPCOT. The first idea for EPCOT (which stood for Experimental Prototype Community of Tomorrow) was a revolutionary new kind of city planned to be built on Disney property. The model for it, now named Progress City, was created to show off Walt's concept. While this vision of EPCOT never materialized, part of the enormous model lives on in Tomorrowland. The dreams of a community of tomorrow do exist, in a fashion, in today's Tomorrowland. The land is themed to represent an intergalactic spaceport, with robots, aliens, and humans commingling in one peaceful society. While Tomorrowland in Disneyland Paris draws inspiration from Jules Verne, the Magic Kingdom's vision of the future is derived from Buck Rogers and Flash Gordon, with campy flying saucers serving as decorations throughout the land.

Flight to the Moon

One portion of the audio on the Tomorrowland Transit Authority PeopleMover honors a former attraction called Flight to the Moon. While traveling through Space Mountain on the PeopleMover, we hear terminal-style announcements saying: "Paging Mr. Morrow, Mr. Tom Morrow. Please contact Mr. Johnson in the control tower to confirm your flight to the moon"—a reference to the animatronic "host" of Flight to the Moon, also wittily named Tom Morrow. This attraction later become Mission to Mars, and then was replaced by Alien Encounter, which in turn gave way to Stitch's Great Escape. The Mr. Morrow animatronic in Mission to Mars was earlier referred to as "Mr. Johnson," so the announcement on the PeopleMover pays double tribute to the character. The general layout of Stitch's Great Escape, and the ExtraTERRORestrial Alien Encounter before it, can be traced directly to Mission to Mars and Flight to the Moon. In the original attraction, the preshow featured an interactive conversation with Mr. Morrow as he stood in the control room. Visitors then moved to one of two circular theaters set up to see viewscreens in the floor, ceiling, and sides of the theater, which captured the action as our rocket ship blasted off, made its way to Mars, and returned home. Today's attraction adds hardware, particularly in the center of the theater and in the interactive seat restraints, but the layout of rooms and even the use of the viewscreens remain largely the same.

Alien Encounter

An Astro Orbiter vehicle alongside the PeopleMover was placed here because of a former Tomorrowland attraction. The Astro Orbiter vehicle visible just after the Progress City model contains an alien about to blast into space. This reference to Tomorrowland's status as a spaceport for aliens dates to 1994, when an attraction called the ExtraTERRORestrial Alien Encounter replaced Mission to Mars. On the occasion of its addition, the entire land was given a facelift and re-conceived as a spaceport. Today's Astro Orbiter replaced a similar ride called Star Jets, which featured a vehicle design with larger wings, as if necessary for planetary re-entry. Without Alien Encounter, Tomorrowland today might still be a disjointed celebration of futurism and space travel without a sense of a specific place like a spaceport.

Opening Date for Stitch's Great Escape

A plaque next to the entrance doors for Stitch's Great Escape may be written with letters that look alien, but they are really just stylized English letters. The plaque commemorates the opening date for the attraction. It reads: "Dedication. This Galactic Federation prisoner teleport center is hereby dedicated to the preservation of peace and harmony throughout the galaxy by protecting the nice from the naughty. The Grand Councilwomen [sic]. 2004 November 16."

Skippy

The second preshow room of Stitch's Great Escape features two teleportation tubes that show different aliens being transported to our location. In the Alien Encounter version of the show, these tubes were used to teleport a single cute critter named Skippy from one end of the room to the other, but a teleportation accident leaves him looking different on the other side. In the current show, the two animatronics are meant to represent completely different beings, but they were once the same character.

X-S Tech

One piece of futuristic equipment visible after the preshow for Stitch's Great Escape still bears the name of a fictional private company from Alien Encounter. The company, X-S Tech (an obvious pun on the reliance on technology), featured heavily in Alien Encounter as the creator of the teleportation technology, but is not explicitly mentioned in Stitch's Great Escape. The machines with this logo can be seen on the right side of the path as visitors head toward the "Level Three" chamber to meet Stitch.

Alien Spaceport

Murals in the Merchant of Venus store call further attention to the alien spaceport concept. Designed to show off the rest of Tomorrowland as if the walls were transparent windows rather than paintings, these murals behind the cash registers show the familiar Tomorrowland architecture and depict Stitch-like aliens wandering about the land. Stitch is specifically referenced even outside the attraction that bears his name. One painted mural at the exit to Buzz Lightyear's Space Ranger Spin features a very small image of the spacecraft from the *Lilo and Stitch* movie. Sharp-eyed patrons will even notice Stitch's footprints on the ceiling of Merchant of Venus.

Timekeeper

The antenna dishes seen in the queue of Monsters Inc. Laugh Floor are holdovers from the previous tenant here. The attraction which preceded Monsters Inc. Laugh Floor was a Circle-Vision movie called Timekeeper, which included a robotic host designed to look like a futuristic robot. Because the audience was time-traveling and the theme of Tomorrowland was one of a spaceport, many design elements emphasized interstellar commerce and communication. The antenna dishes in the Timekeeper queue made thematic sense then, but less so with the Monstropolis theme.

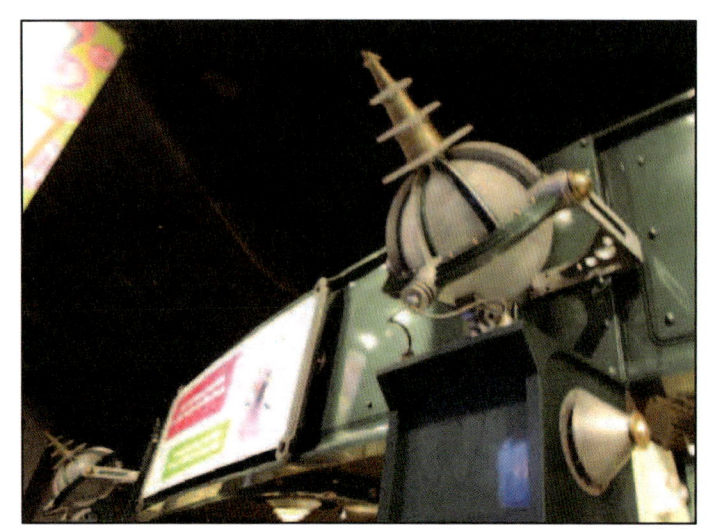

Circle-Vision 360

The curved back wall of the Monsters, Inc. Laugh Floor is a structural remnant of the original occupant here, the Circle-Vision 360 theater. Films such as *America the Beautiful* and *Magic Carpet 'Round the World* played here starting in 1971, and the Circle-Vision theater remained untouched for the Timekeeper replacement starting in 1994. The transition to the Monsters Inc. Laugh Floor brought many changes to the building's décor, but the circular shape of the main room was dictated by the building's fundamental structure, designed long ago for the Circle-Vision movies.

Imagineer Chuck Ballew

The mural in the queue of Buzz Lightyear's Space Ranger Spin contains an inside joke left by the artist. The painter, Chuck Ballew, named one of the planets on the mural after himself, here disguised as planet Chokball.

Dreamflight

A set piece in Buzz Lightyear's Space Ranger Spin is left unaltered from the previous attraction in this location. The rotating red light amid fog just prior to the theater-like finale of Buzz Lightyear is actually a remnant from the previous inhabitant, Dreamflight, which was also known as Take Flight for many years. This set was originally meant to signify our vehicles entering a giant turbine engine, as the ride was first sponsored by Eastern Airlines, then Delta Airlines. The red frame overhead as we enter the area still remains, though it is now labeled an escape hatch. One other feature remains from the old track layout: the "speed tunnel" near the end of the attraction was left intact, but given a new film so riders could blast the projection of Zurg's spaceship. The Buzz Lightyear attraction uses the same drive mechanism and even the entire track layout is unaltered from Take Flight—which had itself been an update of the original attraction here, If You Had Wings. Visitors on the PeopleMover now peer into one room of Buzz Lightyear's Space Ranger Spin, but when Dreamflight occupied this space, they could glance down on both sides of the PeopleMover track and see into separate rooms. These days, unused windows on the left side of the PeopleMover track give testament to the location where visitors used to sneak a peak at the second room. Wooden cutouts of chickens in Buzz Lightyear's Space Ranger Spin also come from the attraction which preceded it. Three chickens just in front of our vehicle in the volcano room of Buzz Lightyear had once occupied the first room of Dreamflight, where whimsical cutout figures celebrated the rural nature of early flight. Another show feature retained from Dreamflight can be seen in the first few scenes (and the very final scene), where cloud-shaped bumps alongside the vehicle track frame what visitors can see near the floor. Now painted black, these billowy humps originally represented clouds, in keeping with the aeronautical theme of Dreamflight.

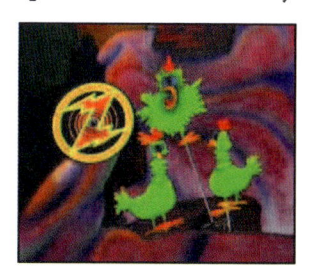

Imagineering Batteries

The cylindrical batteries seen throughout Buzz Lightyear's Space Ranger Spin contain their own inside joke: they are "Made in Glendale," a reference to the home of Walt Disney Imagineering in Glendale, California. Additional versions of these batteries can also be seen in the attraction's queue and exit area.

The Tomorrowland Times

One of the static robot statues in Tomorrowland under the PeopleMover displays a remnant from a former time in Tomorrowland. While the Galaxy Gazette seems to be the current newspaper being "sold" by this robot, the former newspaper was called the Tomorrowland Times (which discussed the transportation technology of X-S Tech as seen in Alien Encounter). A small portion of the Tomorrowland Times can still be glimpsed through the window of the robot's chest, in a detail that was never updated when Stitch took over Alien Encounter.

Carousel of Progress Sponsor

Walt Disney's Carousel of Progress displays many hints of its original sponsor even long after its sponsorship ended. Conceived for the 1964 World's Fair in New York, the original show (then called Progressland) was sponsored by General Electric, and was designed to show how the company and its household appliances had made life easier over the century. While the narration was adjusted and no longer invoked General Electric by name, the appliances themselves are still present, many are labeled with the GE brand, and some are even animated and still form a central part of the show's theme of progress over the decades. Two of the most prominent are a vacuum cleaner in the 1920s and a refrigerator in the 1940s.

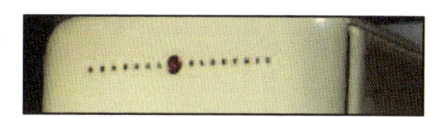

WDI Symbols

Walt Disney Imagineering uses Sorcerer Mickey (from *Fantasia*) as its corporate logo, and the blue sorcerer hat with white stars and moons in particular as its symbols. These symbols appear in two places in Carousel of Progress. In the 1940s set, look to the right of the daughter's exercise machine to spy the familiar sorcerer's hat with the stars and moon. In the finale scene, set your gaze on two show plates high above the far-right corner to see a more subtle design of white stars and moons on a blue background.

Imagineer Herb Ryman

Longtime Disney artist Herb Ryman, who created many conceptual paintings of Disney theme parks and their attractions, is honored in the second scene of Carousel of Progress (the 1920s). His tribute comes in the form of a billboard in the cityscape seen through the window, which proclaims "Herb Ryman – Attorney at Law." Ryman was the artist who helped Walt create a critical early painting of Disneyland to sell the idea of the park when he needed funding.

Glendale Street Address

A handwritten note on the dry-erase board in the finale scene of Carousel of Progress pays tribute to the division of the company that designs and builds the theme parks. Walt Disney Imagineering (WDI) is based out of 1401 Flower Street in Glendale, California, so the mention of 1401 (ostensibly, the flight number for grandma and grandpa) is no coincidence.

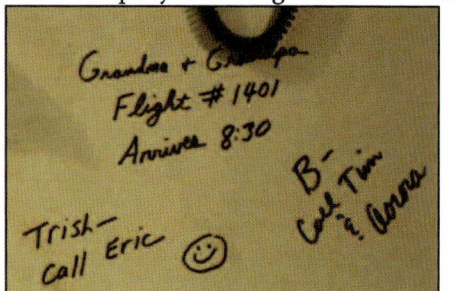

Imagineer Marty Sklar

A note stuck to a corkboard in the final scene of Carousel of Progress makes an inside joke about the management of Walt Disney Imagineering. This last scene features a modern household, and far off to the right sits a board where notes and reminders are posted. One prominent note reads "Marty called – wants changes!" This might sound like a reference to a document someone is working on, but is an inside joke to the Imagineers. "Marty" refers to Marty Sklar, who for decades was the head of WDI, and a person one could well imagine calling to ask for changes to rides!

Space Mountain History

The list of "Active Earth Stations" in the first room of Space Mountain's queue includes references to all versions of Space Mountain from around the globe. Sometimes the locations are listed more obviously (Tokyo and Paris), while Anaheim is referenced by its opening date of 1977 and Hong Kong's makes an oblique reference to "E-TKT" or E-Tickets.

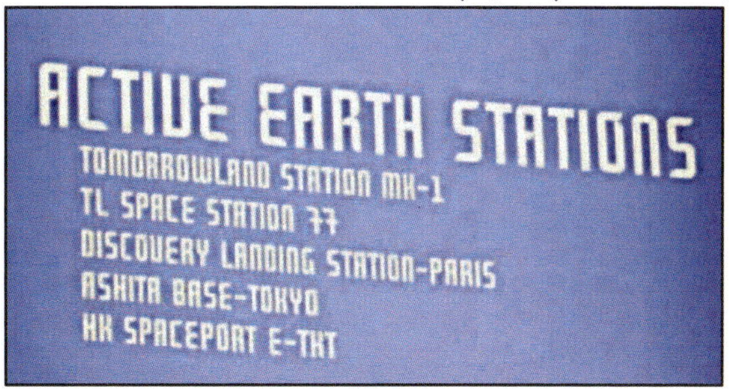

Hyperion Studios

A lighted mural in the queue of Space Mountain includes a reference to one of the earliest locations for the Walt Disney Studios. The second mural mentions the term "Hyperion," which is significant in the history of the Disney company. Before the animation studio moved to its present home in Burbank (after the 1937 success of *Snow White and the Seven Dwarfs*), it was located in Hollywood on 2719 Hyperion Avenue.

Space Mountain Opening Date

Space Mountain's opening date of 1975 is commemorated on the attraction's logo. It was built in the 1970s as the world's first enclosed roller-coaster to operate in the dark, preceding even its cousin in Anaheim.

Imagineer John Hench

A longtime artist at the Walt Disney Studios and one of the key Imagineers to build Disneyland and Walt Disney World, John Hench was chosen by Walt to create the first visions of Space Mountain back in the 1960s. The front pod of the spaceship over our heads on the lifthill is labeled H-NCH, a clear reference to John Hench. The year 1975 is referenced alongside Hench's name.

Closed Magic Kingdom Rides

The robot console at the start of the exit speedramp to Space Mountain includes a section labeled "Space Tug Dispatch" (in the lower-left of the console) that makes reference to several closed attractions and other newly-added attractions. The "Open Sectors" (in other words, rides added) list uses abbreviations (such as FL-MAWP) to refer to Many Adventures of Winnie the Pooh, Aladdin's Flying Carpets, Mickey's Philharmagic, Splash Mountain, Buzz Lightyear's Space Ranger Spin, and Monsters Inc. Laugh Floor. The list of "Closed Sectors" (i.e., closed rides, also using abbreviations) includes 20,000 Leagues, Mr. Toad's Wild Ride, Skyway to Fantasyland, Swan Boats, Mickey Mouse Revue, and Mission to Mars.

Florida Freeways

The top-left console at the beginning of the exit speedramp makes mention of several local roads in Central Florida. A1-A is a road along the Atlantic coast, while Interstate-4 (I4) sits right next to Walt Disney World and often has heavy congestion. US-192 is the road on the other border of Walt Disney World, which has many motels and restaurants, as it is a tourist zone.

Space Mountain Sponsor

A mechanical dog was crafted as a subtle reference to the attraction's original sponsor, RCA. The mascot for RCA was Nipper, who was famous for his trademark cocked head and floppy ears. When FedEx took over as sponsor of the ride in the 1990s, they created the dioramas still visible today at the exit to the ride and included a mechanical dog crafted for the original sponsor. These dioramas were originally meant to represent far-flung corners of the galaxy, places to which FedEx would ship packages. The control center at the start of the moving sidewalk was originally labeled as a shipping center. FedEx ceased its sponsorship in 2004, and the scenes were later re-themed to vacation destinations rather than created anew.

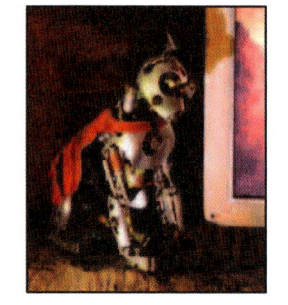

Mesa Verde

Stickers on "luggage" in the post-show to Space Mountain pay homage to previous attractions that celebrated the future. Stickers include Mesa Verde, the fictional "future city" that was one of the possible endings on Epcot's former ride Horizons, as well as Space Station X-1, which had been an early exhibit in Anaheim's Tomorrowland in 1955.

Sonny Eclipse

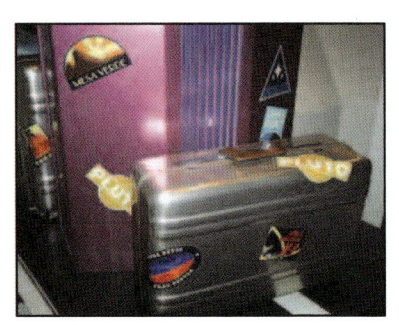

Sonny Eclipse, the robotic performer in Cosmic Ray's Starlight Café, is physically a duplicate of Officer Zzyxx, an alien in Tokyo Disneyland that greets visitors in a restaurant called the Pan Galactic Pizza Port. Tokyo's Pan Galactic Pizza Port is referenced a second time in Orlando's Tomorrowland, on a sign glimpsed very briefly from the PeopleMover. Following the model of Progress City on the left, a darkened space displays several neon-accented posters that are illuminated by black light. One of the posters announces "hot delivery" of Pan Galactic Pizza "right to your planet."

Former Ticket Booth

Until EPCOT Center opened in 1982, most attractions at Walt Disney World required tickets to ride (ranked A through E), and kiosks were used to sell additional tickets. One such ticket booth in Tomorrowland is now used to advertise the Disney Vacation Club.

Indianapolis Speedway

The Tomorrowland Speedway's former sponsor left traces behind when it departed in 2009. Originally named the Grand Prix Raceway, it offered an international car race. It later became the Tomorrowland Indy Speedway, in honor of the Indianapolis 500 race that sponsored the attraction. The popular race car ride lost its sponsor and most of the decorations in 2009, but one prominent element from the Indy sponsorship remained. A row of bricks marking the start line was meant as an homage to the famous "yard of bricks" at the Indianapolis Motor Speedway, where the track surface was long ago entirely covered with 3.2 million bricks, but 3 feet of original bricks remained at the start line. Having a row of symbolically-significant bricks at the start line was a concept brought over to Orlando as well, and the tribute remains today.

Original Timothy

The Timothy Mouse figure at the entrance to Dumbo was an original prop from the original Dumbo attraction. Before Dumbo moved to its present location, it was situated directly behind the carousel and the castle, and it was a single spinner ride rather than two. Atop that spinner was the Timothy Mouse prop, now seen on the sign for Dumbo.

Casey Jr. Homage

The numbers on the Casey Jr. engine and the nearby merchandise cart pay tribute to the original Casey Jr. train attraction at Disneyland. In Anaheim, there are only two train engines, numbered 7 and 9. In Orlando, there is only the one train (which is the stationary water playground). Designers elected to give the stationary train the number 9, leaving the number 7 unused in their tribute so far, so it was added to the merchandise cart as a nod to Disneyland.

Park Opening Years

The circus wagons at Casey Jr. Splash 'N' Soak are labeled with the opening years of the four Walt Disney World parks: 71 (for Magic Kingdom), 82 (for EPCOT Center), 89 (for Disney-MGM Studios), and 98 (for Disney's Animal Kingdom).

Disneyland's Opening Year

One of the circus wagons serving as a snack stand near Casey Jr. Splash 'N' Soak honors Disneyland by listing its opening year (1955) as the wagon's identifying number.

Firehouse Five Plus Two

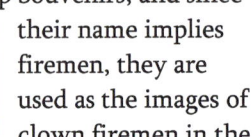

Various locations in Storybook Circus honor a jazz band comprised of animators from the Walt Disney Studios from the 1950s. Firehouse Five Plus Two achieved national fame via televised appearances, and their most prominent member was Imagineer Ward Kimball, who was also instrumental in re-kindling Walt Disney's interest in trains (and eventually, Disneyland). The band is mentioned by name on fire extinguisher boxes inside Big Top Souvenirs, and since their name implies firemen, they are used as the images of clown firemen in the Dumbo waiting room playground and on the circus wagons of Casey Jr. Soak 'n' Splash. Look in particular for Ward Kimball, who is always depicted with sturdy black, round eyeglasses.

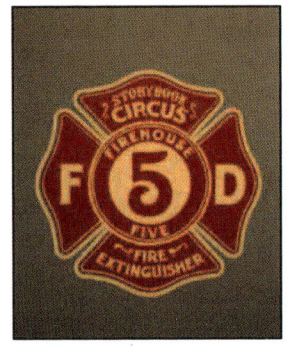

Luxo Ball

The Pixar corporate symbol, a bouncing ball with a distinctive star pattern and red, yellow, and blue coloring, appears on tables in the Storybook Circus dining area as a further way to make this area seem familiar even to newcomers and to help shrink the Disney universe.

Carolwood Pacific Railroad

The sign at the Storybook Circus train station pays homage to Walt Disney's backyard railroad, which he nicknamed the Carolwood Pacific Railroad because his home was on Carolwood Dr. in Holmby Hills, CA. A second mention of Carolwood can be spotted just outside the nearby restrooms, where a panel on one wall also invokes the name.

Barnstormer at Goofy's Wiseacre Farm

The Barnstormer was renamed in 2012 with the opening of Storybook Circus. The ride had previously been here during the years of Mickey's Toontown Fair, when it was known as The Barnstormer at Goofy's Wiseacre Farm. It honors the old ride by including Goofy's pants atop the new sign (his pants were used as a windsock in the old attraction) and by painting the backside of the new marquee sign as though the boards had been re-used and re-arranged from the old sign. If you squint and use your imagination, you can just make out the lettering from the old sign.

20,000 Leagues Squid

The weathervane atop the DVC facility in the Little Mermaid section of Fantasyland offers a subtle call-out to a former ride in this location. The climax of the submarine-themed attraction once in this exact spot, 20,000 Leagues Under the Sea, was a battle with a giant squid. To commemorate the attraction, the weathervane of a giant squid was added atop the DVC building.

Mapmaker Harper Goff

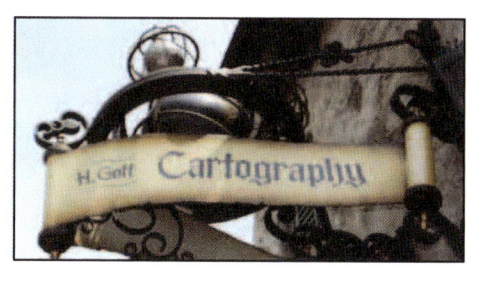

Disney Imagineer Harper Goff, who created many of the first concept art maps for Disneyland and Walt Disney World, is credited as the cartographer at the Fantasyland DVC booth. Goff was instrumental in creating the look of the film *20,000 Leagues Under the Sea*, which had helped create the steampunk look that influences the DVC booth.

Under the Sea Name

The name of the Little Mermaid attraction, Under the Sea, is both a reference to one of the movie's signature songs and a tribute to the submarine ride that preceded it here in Orlando. The Mermaid ride in California, which opened first, did not use the same subtitle—there, it is known as Ariel's Undersea Adventure. So the revising of the name in Orlando to "Under the Sea" points to the tribute-like nature of this name, as the original sub ride was called 20,000 Leagues Under the Sea. Just like that submarine ride, Ariel's attraction features plenty of starfish and barnacles alongside the walls (in the sub ride, this is what you saw out of the portholes at the start and end of the ride), as well as a curtain of bubbles as we "submerge."

Nautilus

A design in the queue for Under the Sea pays tribute to the attraction which preceded it on this spot. A line carving in the rocks near the water line at one pool traces the outline of the Nautilus, the submarine at the heart of 20,000 Leagues Under the Sea attraction in Fantasyland.

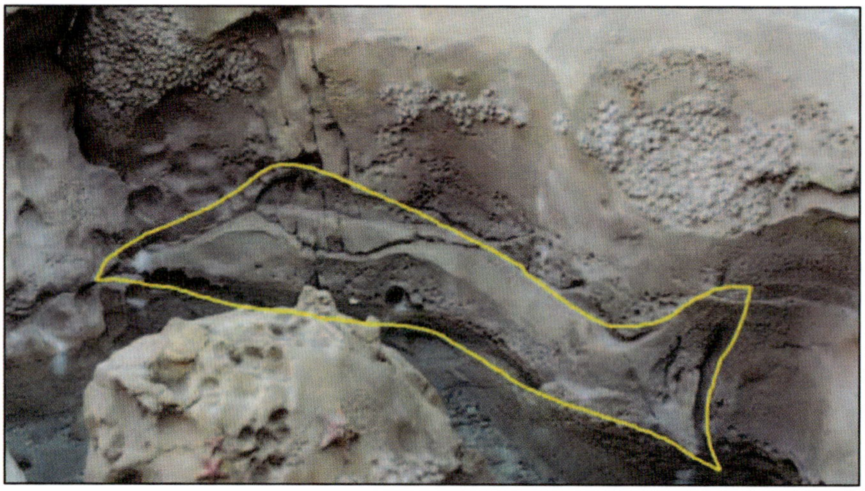

Snow White's Scary Adventures

The vultures at the top of the lift hill in the Seven Dwarfs Mine Train are props once used in the Snow White's Scary Adventures dark ride. This original ride from the Magic Kingdom's earliest days showed events from the movie roughly in order, and was closed in 2012 to make room for Princess Fairytale Hall. The two vultures were perched atop a tree near the climax of the attraction, and helped guide riders' eyes to the right up the mountain to see the dwarfs lined up to take on the Queen. Several of the dwarf figures at the end of the coaster, seen in the cottage, are also re-used from the former dark ride attraction. Bashful, Doc, Grumpy, Happy, and Sleepy are recycled; Dopey and Sneezy had to be created anew for their dancing position in the new attraction.

Magic Kingdom Vice President Phil Holmes

The executive in charge of the Magic Kingdom in the year when New Fantasyland opened is memorialized via a portrait in Bonjour Village Gifts. Phil Holmes had been with the Magic Kingdom since its opening day (he worked at the Haunted Mansion in 1971) and risen to its top position by 2012. Numerous winks in the painting pay tribute to changes during his tenure: a ring with "40" stamped on it (the 40th anniversary of the park in 2011), Aladdin's lamp (the addition of Magic Carpets of Aladdin), Snow White's apple (the closure of Snow White's Scary Adventures), peanuts (for the addition of Storybook Circus), bronze statue of Donald Duck (the trinket given to Cast Members when they pass 40 years of service), and a map of the Magic Kingdom showing Mickey's Toontown Fair (the first land to close).

Imagineer Babies

The cherubs on the ceiling of Be Our Guest restaurant's central ballroom dining area are representations of the children of the Imagineers who worked on the project. Most European palaces with such frescoes feature angels and cherubs only of white European descent, but the cherubs in Be Our Guest are multi-racial because the Imagineers on the project were themselves diverse.

Imagineer Randy Pausch

One artificial leaf blade at the Mad Tea Party offers a quote by a noted Imagineer who died young. The fanciful display of an actual tea party amid the shrubs near the attraction has an oversized leaf with an inscription that reads "Be good at something; it makes you valuable…. Have something to bring to the table, because that will make you more welcome. – Randy Pausch." Randy had been an Imagineer for many years, and found fame late in life as a Carnegie Mellon professor who was offered the chance to participate in the "Last Lecture" series of uplifting speeches, which challenged faculty to give a speech as though it was their last lecture ever to deliver to students, as a way of measuring what's really important in life. Shortly before delivering his planned Last Lecture, Randy discovered he was really terminally ill, which caused him to rethink the contents of that now truly Last Lecture. He turned the occasion into a bestselling book, and when he died, he was honored at Walt Disney World with this inspirational quote.

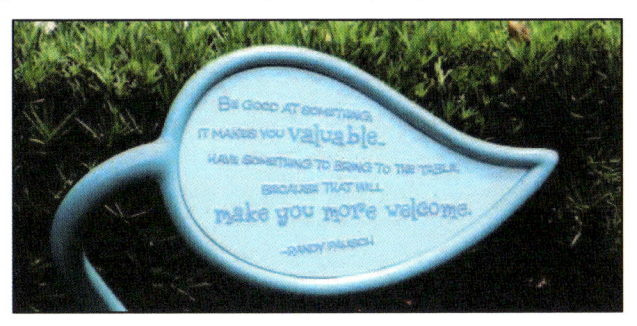

Mr. Toad's Wild Ride

A painting in the Many Adventures of Winnie the Pooh honors the former occupant of this space, Mr. Toad's Wild Ride. That former ride used characters from the Disney movie *The Wind in the Willows*, including Mr. Toad, Moley, Winky, and others. In today's attraction, the left wall of Owl's house features paintings, one of which shows Mr. Toad handing a piece of paper marked "DEED" over to Owl, implying a transfer of this property from Toad to Winnie the Pooh and his pals. A second painting on the opposite side of the room has "fallen" onto the floor showing Moley, another character from Mr. Toad's Wild Ride, standing with Winnie the Pooh. A third painting, back on the left side of the vehicle in the same room, shows Owl smiling through a handlebar moustache in a tribute to Winky, yet another character from the Toad movie and attraction. To top it off, in this picture Owl is wearing a skimmer straw hat, just like Toad was at the end of his movie.

20,000 Leagues Under the Sea

The tree and its playhouse outside the Many Adventures of Winnie the Pooh pay tribute to the ride which once dominated Fantasyland. Visitors who step inside the room carved out of the base of Pooh's tree will notice a sleek, faded green shape above the doorway, visible only from the inside. This is meant to represent a submarine, for the area was once home to a fleet of half-submerged subs that traveled through a lagoon in an attraction called 20,000 Leagues Under the Sea, loosely based on Disney's 1954 movie of the same name. This tree was built for Pooh's Playful Spot, a temporary playground built on the former location of 20,000 Leagues Under the Sea. When Fantasyland underwent renovations in 2010, the tree moved across the sidewalk to its present location. The Nautilus is now a unique tribute, meant for one location but out of place in its current home.

Opening Year in Roman Numerals

A sign above the Friar's Nook announces it was established in MLXXI, or 1071. This matches the medieval setting but still makes an oblique reference to October, 1971, when the Magic Kingdom first opened. At various times in its history, this location was called Lancer's Inn, Gurgi's Munchies & Crunchies, Lumiere's Kitchen and Village Fry Shoppe.

Disney Coat of Arms

A coat of arms on the back side of Cinderella Castle displays the Disney symbol of three lions (one of six coat of arms associated with the name Disney). This same coat of arms adorns Sleeping Beauty Castle in Anaheim's Disneyland.

Imagineer Dorothea Redmond

Dorothea Redmond, the artist who designed the tile mosaics of Cinderella in the pass-through walkway left her signature, in the form of mosaics in one lower corner of the walkway. Mentioned with Redmond is artist Hanns Scharff, who created the mosaic. Scharff gained initial notoriety for being the master interrogator of the German Luftwaffe during WWII; he later directed his efforts to art in general and mosaics in particular. Scharff's daughter in law, Monika, assisted with the mosaic, as well as the twin mosaics outside the Land pavilion in Epcot. Dorothea Redmond was also the creator of the apartment suite for Walt Disney in California, which was to go in the space above Pirates of the Caribbean. Since Walt Disney died before completion, that area in California was used for the Disney Gallery for many years, until it was converted to the Dream Suite for special events and visitors in 2008.

Coats of Arms

Coats of arms in Cinderella's Royal Table, the restaurant inside Cinderella Castle, honor people important to the Disney organization. Coats of arms scattered throughout the interior of the castle, especially the waiting area and the main dining room of the restaurant, refer to the family names of many individuals who helped design and make the Disney theme parks a reality. Some of these symbols are also visible on the stained glass windows and can be seen from the outside of the castle, in the courtyard that is home to the carrousel.

Disney Family Apartment

A large space was set aside in the upper areas of Cinderella Castle when it was first built to serve as an apartment for the Disney family, but it was never fully built or decorated until the 2007 promotion "Year of a Million Dreams." Finally outfitted with furniture and lavish trappings, the "Dream Suite" apartment remains off-limits for normal public viewing. Visitors on the outside can catch a glimpse, though, by looking at the castle from the back side and spying three stained-glass windows 2/3rds of the way up the castle, off to one side.

Sword in the Stone Ceremony

A sword stuck in an anvil in the Fantasyland courtyard was once part of a brief live show involving visitors. Until 2006, several times per day characters from the Disney movie *The Sword in the Stone* would appear and encourage children to try to yank the sword from the anvil. A Cast Member observing from afar would trigger the lock to finally allow the sword to budge, though not fully come free, and a new ruler was crowned.

Miss Liberty

Carved figures atop Prince Charming Regal Carrousel are remnants of this ride's first incarnation. When it was first built in 1917 for the Detroit Palace Garden Park, it was named Miss Liberty and painted patriotic colors. It was purchased in 1967 in Maplewood, New Jersey, and fully reconditioned and repainted for inclusion in the Magic Kingdom.

Mickey Mouse Revue

Mickey Mouse's role as conductor in Mickey's Philharmagic harkens back to a previous attraction at this very location. Before Mickey's Philharmagic opened in 2003, this space was occupied by a live-action puppet show called Legend of the Lion King. Before that, it was the Fantasyland Theater, which showed a 3-D movie called Magic Journeys. Until 1980, this space was home to the Mickey Mouse Revue, a musical show performed by minimalist animatronics of Disney characters, singing songs led by none other than bandleader Mickey Mouse. Other reminders include the posters in the queue for Mickey's Philharmagic, which includes the Three Little Pigs and the Three Caballeros, two acts which had had roles in the Mickey Mouse Revue. This show was moved in its entirety to Tokyo Disneyland, where it played until 2009. The figures of the seven dwarves were duplicated for the 1994 refurbishment of Snow White's Scary Adventures. Surprisingly, this was not the only instance of recycling the figures from this show. The Alice character, the Mad Hatter, the March Hare, and some flower heads were also removed and taken to Disneyland in 1984, for the major refurbishment of Fantasyland on the West Coast.

Disney Fire Chief Richard LaPere Jr.

A wooden barrel at the exit to Peter Pan's Flight is labeled "Fire Chief Richard LaPere Jr., Lost Boys Fire Brigade." In reality, LaPere is the chief of the real fire department in Walt Disney World, the semi-governmental agency Reedy Creek Improvement District. A similar homage to LaPere can be found near the exit to Big Thunder Mountain Railroad.

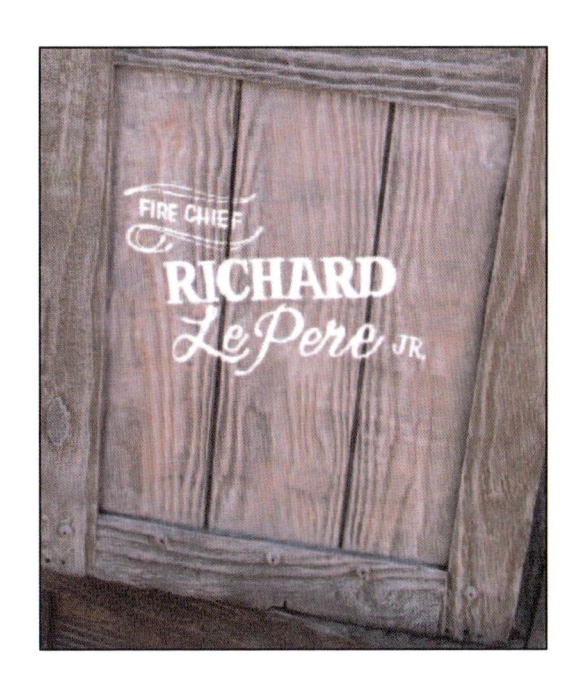

Imagineer Joyce Carlson

One doll in "it's a small world" pays tribute to an artist partly responsible for the ride's look and feel. Joyce Carlson, an Imagineer who assisted in creating the original ride when it premiered at the 1964 World's Fair and later Disneyland, is represented as a doll underneath the Eiffel Tower early in the attraction. Joyce was later placed in charge of installing and maintaining the other versions of the ride around the globe, including the Orlando one. Like Joyce herself, her doll sports big black glasses. The tradition of using a doll to honor the architects of this attraction began at Disneyland, where a doll meant to represent Mary Blair, the primary designer on "it's a small world" and an artist whose distinctive look also graces the murals near the Monorail stop at the Contemporary Resort, can be seen halfway up the Eiffel Tower in California's version of the ride. This doll sports the same yellow coat and black pants which were Mary's trademarks. Even beyond this attraction, there is a long tradition of homages to Disney artists in the finished rides.

Imagineer Leota Thomas

The bronze decorations atop the spires of "it's a small world" are exact copies of one Imagineer's jewelry. Leota Thomas (born Leota Toombs) is well-known to park enthusiasts as Madame Leota in the Haunted Mansion. Her performance as the séance madam was originally intended to be a demonstration only, but designers realized a professional actress would not be able to improve on her performance. She was also known internally at Walt Disney Imagineering for her unique jewelry and earrings. When the Disneyland version of "it's a small world" was being prepared, the sometimes fantastical earrings, pendants, and charms of its chief designer provided a sudden inspiration for the tops of the spires visible on the outdoor façade for the Anaheim attraction. The designs of her jewelry were simply copied and produced on a much larger scale for the attraction's façade. In the Orlando version of the attraction, these bronze toppings look especially like the stud earrings that inspired them, possibly because visitors exit the ride by walking through the spires and thus approach the decorations much more closely than in Anaheim.

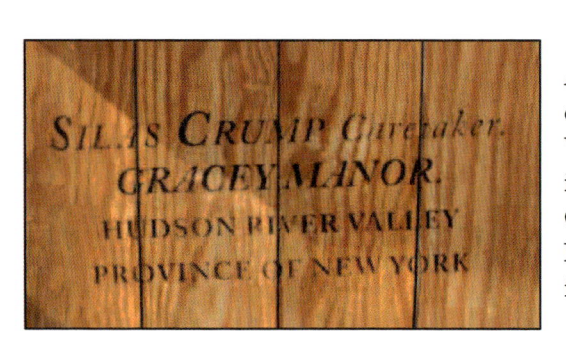

Imagineer Yale Gracey

A crate outside the queue for Haunted Mansion pays tribute to one of its designers. Yale Gracey, the master illusion-maker at WDI, is mentioned on the crate near the line, which also folds in a mention of conceptual artist Rolly Crump: "Silas Crump, Caretaker / Gracey Manor / Hudson River Valley / Province of New York." The Haunted Mansion is meant to represent estates from the Hudson River Valley in New York.

MK Opening Year

A reference to 1971—the year the Magic Kingdom first opened—shows up yet again on a sign just outside the Haunted Mansion. The "Counting House" stenciled sign is part of a location providing information on DVC, the Disney timeshares, and its sign bears the date 1771 across the top.

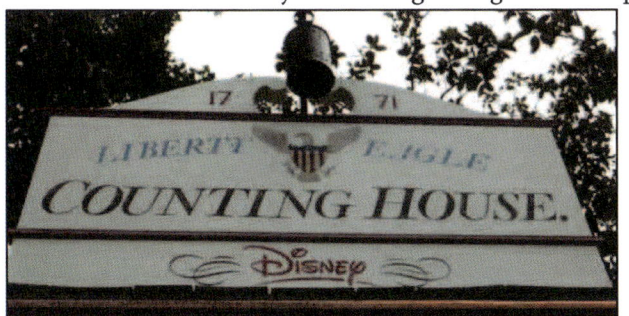

Imagineer Tombstones

Tombstones alongside the queue for the Haunted Mansion honor the Imagineers who helped build the ride. The designers given a tribute here include Xavier Atencio, who wrote the lyrics and script for the show; Marc Davis, who was one of the main creative forces; Yale Gracey, who created many of the illusions; Wathel Rogers, who crafted many of the mechanical effects; Claude Coats, who designed the track layout; Cliff Huet, who was an interior designer; Gordon Williams, who worked with the Audio-Animatronics; Harriet Burns, who designed costumes for the figures; Bob Sewell and Dave Burkhart, who crafted many of the models; Bud Martin, a vice president at WED at the time; Chuck Myall, Fred Joerger, and Bill Martin, who were art directors on the attraction; and Leota Toombs, who performed as the séance madam. The Leota tombstone just outside the entrance to the Mansion was the brainchild of Jason Surrell, an Imagineer so enamored with the Haunted Mansion that he wrote a book about the attraction, its history, and its transformation into a live-action motion picture. Every few seconds, the eyes of the face on this tombstone flutter open, look about, then close again. Many names were added in the 2011 expansion to the queue, including Harper Goff, Roland Crump, and Ken Anderson (conceptual artists), Paul Frees (voice of the Ghost Host), Blaine Gibson (Audio-Animatronics) and Collin Campbell (artwork for the CD re-release).

Thurl Ravenscroft

Voice talent Thurl Ravenscroft, known the world over as the voice of Tony the Tiger, is honored with his name on the interactive organ in the queue of the Haunted Mansion. Ravenscroft had a connection to this ride as he led the musical group the Mellomen and sang the "Grim Grinning Ghosts song" in the finale of the attraction—in fact, it is Thurl's face on the broken marble bust in the graveyard. Thurl was also the voice of Buff the Buffalo in the Country Bear Jamboree.

Internet Fandom's Ring

A wedding ring embedded in the concrete in front of the Ravenscroft organ is a tribute to a remnant that never was. For much of the attraction's history, diehard fans believed that a metal ring stuck in the ground at the exit to the Haunted Mansion was an intentional part of the storyline to the attraction (ostensibly, the bride rejected the dead groom by hurling her ring out the window so that it landed outside), and the Internet fueled the rumor mercilessly about the origins of this ring in the concrete. The metal was originally nothing more than a broken-off piece of a queue pole, with no connection to the ride or its story, but fans were upset when the flagstones were finally replaced to remove the ring, and so when the expanded queue was created a few years later, a variant of the ring in the concrete was added to satisfy the fans looking for this not-quite-official portion of the storyline.

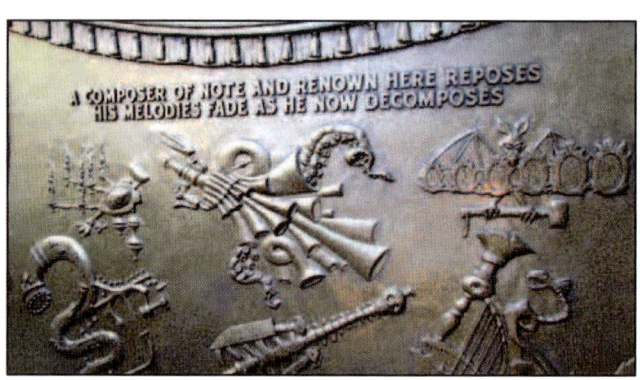

Imagineer Rolly Crump

The touch-sensitive objects on the metal wall of the Haunted Mansion queue are designs originally created by Imagineer Rolly Crump for the various haunted house concepts originally conceived. Rolly's objects often featured nightmarish creations that mashed up inanimate objects (candelabras, torches) with human features (hands, eyes). Most of Rolly's visions never made it to the finished Haunted Mansion, but a few did, and these objects on the second touch-wall represent further designs that never made the cut previously.

Imagineer Ralph Harper Goff

Imagineer Harper Goff gets yet another nod in the Haunted Mansion queue, this time at the bottom of the scroll in an interactive window that encourages visitors to shout a rhyme to complete a poem. The "spectrecom" as it's called is listed as having been patented by R.H. Goff, which uses the initial's of Harper's born name, Ralph Harper Goff.

Happy Haunting Grounds

The movable books that jut out from the bookshelf in the Haunted Mansion queue are labeled with symbols which, when cracked on a 1-for-1 code for the English alphabet, string together several of the taglines associated with marketing the Haunted Mansion over the years into a poem:

Welcome home, you foolish mortals / This mansion is your mystic portal /
Where eerie sights and spooky sounds / Fill these happy haunting grounds.

Mr. Toad's Tombstone

Just outside the exit to the Haunted Mansion, a graveyard ostensibly for pets includes statues and grave markers for dogs, cats, and birds. Back in the far left corner, a humble statue of Mr. Toad himself provides a whimsical tribute to this character, who is "dead" because his ride can no longer be found at the Magic Kingdom after it was replaced by a dark ride dedicated to Winnie the Pooh.

Haunted Mansion's Original Narrator

Many times Guests hear the voice of the Ghost Host, the raven is nearby. In the original plans for the attraction, the bird was supposed to be the Ghost Host, the narrator of the ride. The raven, long associated with death in several cultures, is present in the conservatory on the moving coffin, in the séance room on the chair, in the Ballroom along the rear wall, right outside the attic, and at the end of the graveyard, just as visitors enter the crypt. The séance hostess, Madame Leota, while not the attraction's narrator, still enjoys an Imagineering pedigree. She is voiced by Elanor Audley (who was also Maleficent in Sleeping Beauty) but the facial acting is done by Imagineer Leota Thomas—hence the name Leota for the character as well.

Mr. Lincoln in the Haunted Mansion

One of the Mansion's creepiest optical effects, the busts in the library that appear to turn their heads in sync as the "Doom Buggies" pass by them, actually owes its existence to Great Moments with Mr. Lincoln, a Disneyland-only forerunner to the Hall of Presidents. Designers happened to pass by a negative mold of the Lincoln head—an inverted cast from which the actual head would be made—when they realized that its inverted nature always resulted in the unnerving effect.

Museum of the Weird

Disembodied arms holding torches at the exit to Haunted Mansion are but one of many remnants of a "Museum of the Weird" concept. There was a Walt-era idea to create a museum in Disneyland's New Orleans Square dedicated to strange, supernatural, and occult items, such as might be found in a gypsy's wagon. These concepts were incorporated into the Haunted Mansion in the form of furniture and trappings of the house that seem to be alive but disembodied or unnatural. Besides the arms holding torches, other examples include the clock striking 13 (watch for a face with fangs, and the clock's pendulum as a tail) or the gypsy-like cart outside Orlando's Haunted Mansion selling merchandise. These designs were all the work of Imagineer Rolly Crump.

Carousel of Progress Grandmother

The ghostly woman in a rocking chair at the Ballroom scene of the Haunted Mansion is a duplicate figure from another attraction. The Audio-Animatronics figure is a duplicate of the grandmother in Carousel of Progress. The first versions of both of these rides were conceived and built in the 1960s, so it made sense to re-use the molds of existing Audio-Animatronics whenever possible.

Voice Actor Thurl Ravenscroft

One of the iconic singing busts in the graveyard scene of the Haunted Mansion shows a video projection of prolific voice actor Thurl Ravenscroft, who lent his deep voice to popular cultural touchstones like Tony the Tiger and *How the Grinch Stole Christmas*. For the Disney parks, Thurl was the voice of parrot Fritz in the Tiki Room, Buff in the Country Bear Jamboree, frogs in Splash Mountain, several pirates in Pirates of the Caribbean, and the lead singer in the song Grim Grinning Ghosts. Thurl's projection is on the broken statue which is sometimes mistaken for Walt Disney's face.

Indoor Tombstones

The tombstones in the finale sequence of the Haunted Mansion, which takes place in the graveyard, also pay tribute to Imagineers on the attraction. In some cases, though, the names of the Imagineers are scrambled. One tombstone near the track pays homage to Judi Gray, Fred Joerger, and Harriet Burns, all model-builders, but their names are listed with the letters in randomized order.

Headless Horseman

The Haunted Mansion is modeled after houses where the Headless Horseman story was set. Houses built in the 18th century in the picturesque Hudson River Valley, now a National Heritage area and home to well-preserved dwellings from several different epochs in American history, provided the thematic inspiration for the general look of the Haunted Mansion. The Hudson River Valley is also the setting for the legend of Sleepy Hollow and the Headless Horseman. At the other end of Liberty Square, an eatery named "Sleepy Hollow Refreshments" provides a thematic bookend for the land. This building was inspired by the real Hudson River Valley house of the Sleepy Hollow author, Washington Irving. Crates in the outdoor dining area mention characters from the story, such as Ichabod Crane and Abraham van Brunt, at the location of "Irving's boarding house." Across the way from Sleepy Hollow Refreshments, a sign states that the proprietor of the music lessons shop is none other than Ichabod Crane, who did a fair amount of singing in the original story. A Headless Horseman can even sometimes be seen at the Magic Kingdom. During Mickey's Not So Scary Halloween Party, a Headless Horseman thunders down the parade route before the party's parade.

Presidential Voices

Many of the modern presidents lend their own voices to the Hall of Presidents attraction. An actor provided the voice for Abraham Lincoln in the early years of the Hall of Presidents, but Bill Clinton was the first sitting president to lend his voice to a speech, and George W. Bush and Barack Obama continued the tradition. The show was renovated and modernized in several ways for its reopening after Obama's inauguration.

Imagineer Faces

Many of the presidents' faces in the Hall of Presidents were created by taking molds of Imagineers. To generate life-like results, molds of actual people were used instead of sculpting them from scratch based only on pictures. Some of the molds were used more than once. John Hench became John Quincy Adams, Herb Ryman became James Monroe, Tony Baxter became James Polk, and Marc Davis became John Adams.

Lincoln-Douglas Debates

Two paintings hanging in the exit lobby of the Hall of Presidents were used in the original version of the show. When a refurbishment was undertaken in 2008, several scenes were cut from the show's movie while others were added. One of the paintings showing Lincoln debating with Douglas was kept for the new show, but the other was not. However, it remained hanging in the post-show corridor.

Walt Disney's Grandfather

A sign outside Ye Olde Christmas Shoppe honors Walt Disney's grandfather. This sign facing the Liberty Bell replica says "Kepple" on it, in honor of Kepple Disney. This shop is themed to represent three different stores combined over time. Differences in furniture colors and styles, as well as highly varied wallpaper styles, point to the implied history of the merchandise location as one that conglomerated out of three different shops. Trinkets atop shelves in each area attest to the previous residents in each shop: a musician, a woodcarver, and a German family identified as Kepple. In fact, the backstory for the shop is what actually happened. The presence of three separate areas in the Christmas Shoppe can be traced to the fact that originally, there were three distinct stores here! The Christmas Shoppe replaced Mlle. Lafayette's Parfumerie, the Silversmith, and Old World Antiques.

Steamboat Original Names

The Liberty Square Riverboat was originally named the Richard F. Irvine. At first there were two steamboats plying the waters of the Rivers of America: the Admiral Joe Fowler and the Richard F. Irvine, named after two company executives who had done much to help build Walt Disney World. A dry-dock accident permanently crippled the Fowler when it was misaligned during the draining of the water, and after it was sidelined, the Irvine was renamed to the Liberty Belle, though park maps refer to it as the Liberty Square Riverboat. To honor the Irvine, one of its life preservers was kept with the original name for several years. To continue the tradition of honoring these men who did so much to help the Disney company, two of the ferries used to transport guests from the Ticket and Transportation Center to the theme park, named Magic Kingdom-1 and Magic Kingdom-2, were renamed to the Admiral Joe Fowler and Richard F. Irvine. A third ferry is named the General Joe Potter, another figure responsible for building Walt Disney World.

Admiral Joe Fowler

Just as the original Irvine was honored with an unaltered life preserver, the original Fowler was likewise kept alive, in the form of its whistle, which was relocated to the fourth locomotive on the Walt Disney World Railroad, the Roy O. Disney.

Canoe Dock

The unused dock near the exit to Big Thunder Mountain Railroad was once used for a canoe attraction. The Davy Crockett Explorer Canoes were guest-powered free floating canoes on the river. They operated until 1994.

Wilson's Cave Inn

Visible only from the steamboat, a show scene of a keelboat in a cave known as Wilson's Cave Inn (a pun on "cave in") honors an actual location in the Midwest. Cave-In-Rock in Illinois, along the banks of the Ohio River, was similarly shaped and had been a hideout and even a tavern—Wilson's Liquor Vault—in the late 1700s. These real river pirates, in turn, inspired a Disney-made Davy Crockett movie in the 1950s that spurred interest in the frontier and made Disneyland a must-visit destination. Keel boats from the Crockett movies were used at Disneyland, and the idea was brought over to the Magic Kingdom years later.

Mike Fink Keelboats

Keelboats were small flat-bottomed boats used for navigating shallow waters, and had been made fashionable by Disney's Davy Crockett movies. The Mike Fink Keel Boats at the Magic Kingdom were located next to the Haunted Mansion. A nearby shop took on relevant names over the years, such as Keelboat Shop, Keelboat Hat Shop, and Ichabod's Landing, but it closed in 1996. The keelboats moved from here in 1998 to another location near Big Thunder Mountain, and eventually closed completely in 2001. Today, the former dock can still be seen along the river near the Haunted Mansion, though it is presently unused.

Park Opening Year in the Wild West

A sign for "Trail Creek Traders" (not an actual establishment; just a façade) references the first year of Magic Kingdom's operation. Since the park opened in 1971, there are no accidental mentions of "71" anywhere in Walt Disney World, and this mention of 1771 is no exception. This sign can be found on the side of the Diamond Horseshoe, near the restrooms.

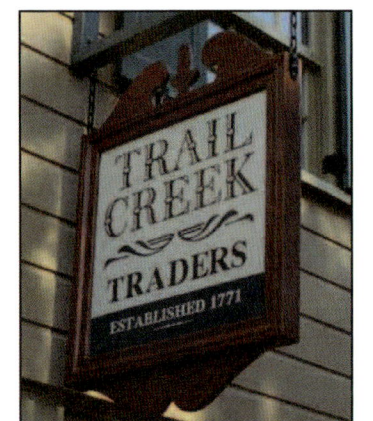

Michael Jackson's Thriller Video

A key visual element of the video to Michael Jackson's *Thriller* (1982)—a hand shooting out of the earth by a tombstone—owes its existence to the shooting gallery at Walt Disney World. Michael admitted to Disney designers that their tombstone in Disneyland and Walt Disney World had inspired the video for him.

Harper's Mill

Harper's Mill, a structure on Tom Sawyer Island named for Imagineer and Studio artist Harper Goff, is home to a unique Disney film reference in the form of a bluebird nest. This is an homage to the Disney cartoon *The Old Mill* (1937), primarily famous today for its introduction of the multiplane camera.

Walt's Childhood Fort

Fort Langhorn on Tom Sawyer Island is a creative descendant of Walt's childhood fort. While watching Walt dictate a revised placement for Fort Wilderness at Disneyland's Tom Sawyer Island, his brother Roy realized that Walt was re-creating a makeshift fort they had often built on a sand bar out on a river as children. Orlando's version, Fort Langhorn, was named after the author Mark Twain, whose real name was Samuel Langhorne Clemens. This fort, once called simply Fort Sam Clemens, can be seen as another recreation of Walt's childhood fort.

Fort Langhorn Cantina

A former counter-service location inside the fort on Tom Sawyer Island has been closed for some years, but the shuttered order windows are still plainly visible, and making their presence even more explicit, there are jars labeled "Provisions" on shelves just above these windows.

Aunt Polly's

Once a quick-service location serving ice cream and smaller snacks on Tom Sawyer Island, Aunt Polly's closed in 2006. It faced the riverboat dock, and its structure, as well as a sign proclaiming Aunt Polly's, can still be seen behind newly-installed vending machines that now block the serving windows.

Disneyland TV Series

The sign for the Frontier Trading Post claims it is run by "Texas John Slaughter"; this is a reference to a similarly-named series on the *Disneyland* TV show from 1958-1961.

Kepple Disney

Walt's grandfather is honored a second time in the Magic Kingdom, courtesy of a mention at the Sorcerers of the Magic Kingdom portal near the pin trading store. There are grain bags on the ground here labeled "Uncle Kepple & Sons Livestock and Feed."

Imagineer Al Bertino

The bear "Big Al" in the Country Bear Jamboree is a loving caricature of one of the show's co-creators, Al Bertino. Together with Marc Davis, Bertino had originally designed this show for use at the planned Mineral Springs Ski Resort in California, though ultimately Walt Disney opted not to develop this property since the infrastructure and roads were not adequate to lure sufficient visitors. This show has had several variations, including the Country Bear Vacation Hoedown (1986-2001) and the Country Bear Christmas Special (1984-2006).

Mine Train Through Nature's Wonderland

The staging of animal encounters on Big Thunder Mountain Railroad pays tribute to the ride which was its creative ancestor. When Big Thunder Mountain Railroad first premiered at Disneyland, it replaced Mine Train Through Nature's Wonderland, a slow-moving train ride through desert scenes and tableaus of robotic animals interacting with their surroundings in various ways. Some of those interactions are recreated at the Magic Kingdom's version of Big Thunder Mountain Railroad. Examples include the bobcat taking refuge from three attacking boars atop a cactus, and a face-off between a roadrunner and a snake, both of which take place in the town of Tumbleweed. The dramatic splashdown at the finale into a dinosaur skeleton was reproduced from Anaheim, where the placing of a skeleton was itself a tribute to a dinosaur skeleton seen during Mine Train Through Nature's Wonderland.

Imagineer Tony Baxter

The portrait of mining magnate Barnabus T. Bullion visible in the Big Thunder queue is a tribute to its original ride designer, Tony Baxter. The painting is an obvious likeness of Baxter, who first conceived the idea of a runaway mine train as part of a Thunder Mesa expansion of Frontierland, originally meant to complement the planned Western River Expedition, but later replaced the concept entirely. Baxter's initials—TWB—were used to create the Big Thunder Mountain logo, with the "W" for Wayne simply inverted to become an "M" in the ride's logo.

Walt-Era Imagineers

The list of names and nicknames on the Fusing Cage in the Big Thunder queue refers to Imagineers active during (and just after) Walt Disney's tenure. These include Blaine Gibson, Stan Jolley, Pat Burke, Clem Hall, Skip Lange, Fred Joerger, Marc Davis, and Helena Hutchinson. Because he joined Tony Baxter early in the project on building the first Big Thunder and was involved in constructing future versions of it, Pat Burke's name also appears on crates inside the ride, most notably overhead in an open-sided shack on the first mid-ride up-ramp.

Western River Expedition

Crates and boxes along the queue of Big Thunder reference the planned Western River Expedition attraction. The slow boat ride through Western River was originally planned as a show heavy in Audio-Animatronics figures, much like Pirates of the Caribbean. This is no coincidence, as originally the Magic Kingdom had no pirates ride (as the Caribbean is not far from Florida) and Western River Expedition was planned to provide an exotic alternative. Guests consistently asked for the familiar pirate ride from Disneyland, however, so Western River Expedition was shelved and Big Thunder Mountain Railroad took its place on the expansion plans.

Park Opening Year

The diagram map of Big Thunder's various mines, seen at the end of the first queue room, includes a mention of the opening year of the park. As we've seen many times already, the Magic Kingdom opened in 1971, so this mention of Shaft #71 in this diagram is no accident.

Rainbow Caverns Mine Train

The diagram map of the ride labels the colorful cave seen in the attraction as "Rainbow Caverns," a nod to the Disneyland ride that preceded Big Thunder at that park in Anaheim. The original ride was slow-moving and climaxed with a trip through colorful stalactites and pools of rainbow-hued water. These designs were echoed intentionally in the eventual Big Thunder attraction (this time at the start of the ride), but the tribute was always informal until the diagram map was added in 2013 and officially labeled the area as Rainbow Caverns.

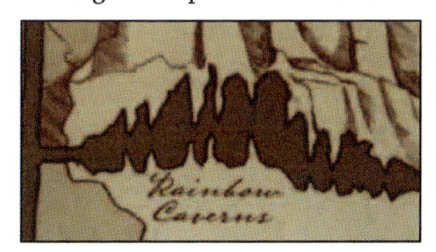

Tony Baxter's Patent

A diagram showing a patent about automatic train braking is attributed to Imagineer Tony Baxter. This diagram shows a Big Thunder engine and car, and is labeled as patent #193,279—this turns out to be a real patent actually about train brakes! Its publication date of July 17, 1877 is faithfully reproduced on this Big Thunder diagram; this patent was selected in the first place because it was about trains and contained a natural reference to July 17 (the day Disneyland opened in 1955).

Tiki Room's Rosita

One birdcage overhead in the second queue room of Big Thunder nods whimsically to its theme park ancestor, the Tiki Room. These birdcages are ostensibly there for the canaries in the mine, used to test the air quality. Rosita as a bird name contains loaded meaning in a Disney park, since there is a bird so named in the Tiki Room. When the birdmobile descends and a roll call of "the girls" is read, host Jose says "I wonder what happened to Rosita," as if she is missing from the roster. The Big Thunder queue elements, added in 2013, finally provided closure to the question— Rosita was used to test the air purity at the mine!

Apple Dumpling Gang

The sign announcing Hard Times Cafe makes oblique reference to the Disney movie *Apple Dumpling Gang*. Imagineer Jason Surrell, who oversaw the Big Thunder queue renovations, was a fan of the movie from the 1970s, which not only was created around the time of the park attraction, but also was set roughly in the same time frame as Frontierland. Another sign earlier in the queue had shown pencil sketches of the two main characters.

Mile Long Bar

The Pecos Bill sign in the Big Thunder queue, in addition to referencing the Disney-created Pecos Bill cartoon, also mentions the Mile Long Bar, a long-gone quick-service bar next to the Pecos Bill-themed eatery in Frontierland. The space formerly used for the Mile Long Bar is today the exit corridor from Country Bear Jamboree.

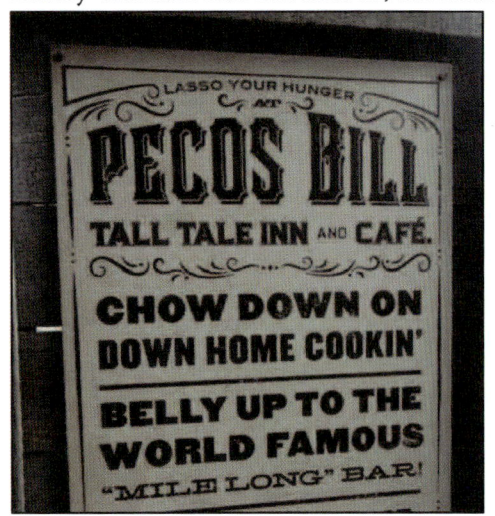

Splash Mountain Gopher

The idea for Disneyland's Splash Mountain was born out of a desire to re-utilize a motley collection of animals from the musical show America Sings, a Tomorrowland attraction that replaced Carousel of Progress in Disneyland and celebrated the history of music in America. Numerous weasels in that show were deployed at Splash Mountain popping up out of gopher holes, implying the same robotic performers were now to be considered gophers! When the Orlando version was built, gophers were newly created. They also duplicated many of the other animals from America Sings rather than create new ones from scratch, including the geese who use fishing poles and the singing frog.

French Fry Cart

A stagecoach wheel just to the right of the Golden Oak Outpost is a remnant and inside joke from the former French Fry cart that preceded the Golden Oak Outpost on this spot. The Golden Oak Outpost was built as a new structure in 2009, but prior to that this area had been home to a smaller cart themed to look like a stagecoach that had broken down and lost one wheel, which was off to the side. The broken wheel was retained as a tribute when the new facility was constructed.

El Pirata y el Perico

One prop high in the rafters at Tortuga Tavern pays tribute to the former name of this restaurant. Until it was renamed and rethemed in 2011, this eatery was known as El Pirata y el Perico (the pirate and the parrot). A cask displaying the original name and logo can still be seen in the ceiling of the outdoor dining room, paying tribute to the history of this location.

Imagineer Marc Davis

One of the major creative forces behind Pirates of the Caribbean, animator and Imagineer Marc Davis is honored at the conclusion of the ride with his family's personal coat-of-arms, displayed high on the exterior wall of the "treasure room" at the very end of the ride.

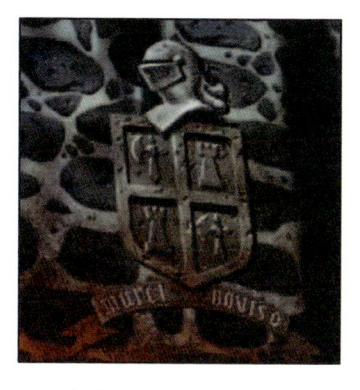

Pirates of the Caribbean Movie Props

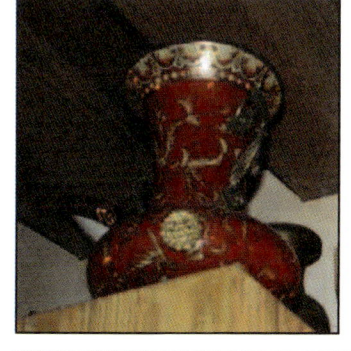

Two items glued to props atop display cases in Plaza Del Sol Caribbe Bazaar, the gift shop at the exit to Pirates of the Caribbean, are artifacts from the *Pirates of the Caribbean* movies. Look for a red china vase atop a display case near the peek-window into the Pirates League boutique; the gold medallion glued to one side here is a prop from the first movie. Across the shop, not far from the restrooms, is a white china vase near the ceiling with a key dangling from it; this key was also a prop from the movies.

Kim Possible World Showcase Adventure

A subtle display in Caribbean Plaza honors the earliest interactive games in the theme parks. Part of the Treasures of the Seven Seas interactive game in Adventureland is a cabinet near the Adventureland crystal shop; midlevel in this crowded cabinet can be found a plate-sized display of artifacts that nod to previous interactive games. There's a dusty and tiny version of the "KP" logo used for the Epcot game, Kim Possible World Showcase Adventure, as well as a tiny platypus skull and fedora in honor of KP's successor, Agent P's World Showcase Adventure. Nearby is also a ribbon and medal in the shape of Sorcerers of the Magic Kingdom, the first interactive game for the Magic Kingdom.

Florida Citrus Growers

Vestiges of the original sponsor remain at the Sunshine Tree Terrace. In its early years, the Tiki Room, then known as the Tropical Serenade, was sponsored by the Florida Citrus Growers. This local association wanted to promulgate the vision of the state as sunny, warm, and welcoming, and it sought to market Florida oranges as superior to all others. It was a natural fit that the association also sponsor the nearby Sunshine Tree Terrace, which served citrus drinks. The association's mascot, the Orange Bird, even maintained a presence at the Magic Kingdom, appearing as both a walkaround character and a figurine in the artificial tree that "sprouted" out of the counter-service location and gave it its name. Although the artificial tree is long gone and the Sunshine Tree Terrace now sports a misleading name, the Orange Bird staged a return in 2012, appearing on the marquee sign and atop a back wall of the serving area. There are also reminders of the association's presence in the décor. Just under the thatched roof is a pattern repeated around the entire structure: a round, orange-colored object, clearly a reference to the citrus fruit which the association wanted to ingrain in people's minds. These painted oranges survived the transition from a sponsor-driven location to a less specific theme. A tribute to Tropical Serenade can be found near the ceiling in Once Upon a Toy at Downtown Disney, as part of a fictional oversized board game.

Elephant Tales

Signs in the shops of Adventureland reference a bygone store. Located in the buildings behind the open-air Agrabah Bazaar, Elephant Tales once housed an upscale clothing store when it opened in 1988. Today, signs with the words "Elephant Tales" can still be seen along a back wall of the Bazaar.

Adventurers Club

Several tags for artifacts in the first part of the Jungle Cruise queue make reference to the Adventurers Club at Pleasure Island. The live-skit and improv comedy show at the Adventurers Club made for a unique form of interactive entertainment, but it closed in 2008. It is no coincidence that Disney's Animal Kingdom shares traits and sensibilities with the Adventurer's Club. One of designer Joe Rohde's first projects for Disney was the Adventurers Club, which presaged his later work at Disney's Animal Kingdom on a number of levels: a mishmash of world cultures, a clutter of artifacts, and a counter-culture vibe in the entire operation. Joe was assisted in designing the Adventurers Club by magician Doug Henning, who crafted the illusions in the show. While 5189 Hill St. isn't the street address of the former comedy club in Pleasure Island, it still has a connection: May 1, 1989 was the opening date of the club, otherwise written as 5/1/89.

Imagineer Wathel Rogers

A sign just inside the entrance to the Jungle Cruise queue pays homage to the Imagineer who gave life to many robotic creations at the Disney parks. Listed on the sign as an animal handler, Wathel Rogers was actually a sculptor who helped create Project Little Man, which led to the development of Audio-Animatronics. He also had a hand in most Audio-Animatronics that followed.

Imagineer Winston Hibler

One barrel in the queue for the Jungle Cruise is addressed to Dr. Winston Hibler, Special Arachnid Unit, Jungle Exploration Company, Outpost #71755. Winston Hibler was the narrator on all the True-Life Adventure films of the 1950s, which largely formed the basis for the Adventureland concept. He was also the unheralded speechwriter for Walt Disney's dedication of Disneyland which opened on July 17, 1955. Hence, the mention of Outpost #71755 acknowledges Hibler's role in Disneyland's grand opening.

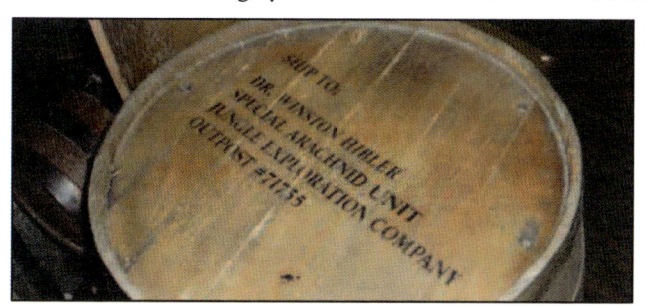

Imagineer Harper Goff

Near the end of the queue at the Jungle Cruise rests a crate labeled "Goff's Brand" of crocodile resistant pants, which pays homage to the main designer of Disneyland's Main Street, Harper Goff. The fictional brand has its ostensible base at "1911 Main Street, Fort Collins, Colorado," a tribute not only to Goff's role in creating Main Street, but also to his hometown of Fort Collins that provided the inspiration for both Disneyland's bank and city hall. Even the supposed street address has significance; 1911 was the year of Goff's birth (he died in 1993).

July 17

An ammo crate in the Jungle Cruise, at the scene where gorillas have overturned a jeep, makes reference to Disneyland's opening in 1955 on July 17. The crate is labeled "Ammo 717"—variations of 7/17 are common throughout the Disney parks to pay homage to the original Disney theme park.

Spartacus

The actor who fought against Kirk Douglas in *Spartacus* lives on at Disneyland and Walt Disney World in the form of the natives seen in the Jungle Cruise. When building the first Jungle Cruise, Imagineer Harper Goff called on Woody Strode, the actor from *Spartacus*, to create a mold of his body from which they could make the needed figures of the natives.

Swiss Family Robinson Director and Actors

Crates at the exit to the Jungle Cruise—near the Swiss Family Treehouse—honor people associated with the book and movie. Kenneth Annakin, the director of the *Swiss Family Robinson* movie, is honored with a crate at the Jungle Cruise exit. The address on this crate makes mention of New Guinea, which was to be the original destination of the Robinsons before they were marooned. A crate just below it is addressed to Johann David Wyss, who authored the original novel, and it is being sent to McGuire Blvd, the joke being that Dorothy McGuire was the actress who played the mother in the movie. There is also a reference to John Mills, the actor who played Father Robinson. The reference to John Mills includes an address on "Bora Danno," a convoluted tribute to James MacArthur, the actor who played son Fritz Robinson. To understand the tribute, one must first know that MacArthur later portrayed Detective Danny Williams in "Hawaii Five-0," the character whose nickname was "Danno."

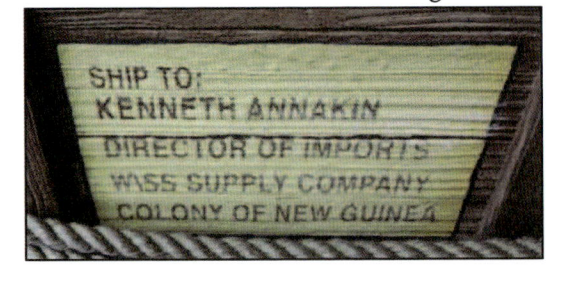

The Oasis

An unused stand at the exit to the Jungle Cruise was once an operational snack stand. Called The Oasis, this location served small food items and juices. Later, it became a merchandise booth, but that too did not last.

Latin Names for Plants and Trees

Throughout the Magic Kingdom, tiny brass plaques announce the scientific Latin names of several varieties of trees, shrubs, and plants. This is a tradition that began in Anaheim's Disneyland and was continued here when the East Coast Magic Kingdom opened up. Originally, it was born out of necessity. As the opening day of Disneyland approached in 1955 and not enough rides and shows were operating, Walt Disney ordered that many of the trees and plants be identified by their Latin names and described in a few sentences, to provide at least an educational exhibit that might make up for the relative lack of attractions on opening day.

Disneyland's Birthday on the Treehouse

There are no accidental occurrences of "July 17" at Disney parks, and the sign at the Swiss Family Robinson pays yet more tribute to the opening of Disneyland in 1955.

Bob Hope

Bwana Bob's was named after comedian Bob Hope, a central figure in Disney theme park history. This store in Adventureland, originally called the "Adventureland Kiosk," was renamed Bwana Bob's in 1985 to honor Bob Hope, who was a personal friend of Walt Disney and who had taken part in Walt Disney World's official opening years before. Bob had starred in a 1963 film named *Call Me Bwana*, which inspired the first half of the store's name. Bob was present at the opening ceremonies for several Disney parks, including Disneyland, the Magic Kingdom, and Disney's Hollywood Studios (then Disney-MGM Studios), where he officially opened the park by cutting the ceremonial opening day ribbon. Bob was heavily involved in one version of the story of Soviet Premier Nikita Khrushchev's desired visit to Disneyland. At a political event Bob paid Disneyland a compliment in conversation with the premier's wife, prompting the premier to try to arrange a visit. When the U.S. Secret Service nixed the idea, saying they couldn't guarantee his safety, Khrushchev's visible anger was televised around the world and became an international incident. Never one to pass up an opportunity—even one he had had an inadvertent hand in creating—Bob Hope turned it into a joke during a performance in Alaska, which he called "halfway between Khrushchev and Disneyland."

SpectroMagic

A figure on a Festival of Fantasy float is a remnant from the former nighttime parade in the Magic Kingdom. From 1991 to 2010 (with some time off in the middle), SpectroMagic was the main nighttime parade, with different music and floats from the Main Street Electrical Parade. The figure of Sebastian now seen on the Little Mermaid float of Festival of Fantasy was a prop used in SpectroMagic. This is not the only holdover in the parade. The Cleo and Figaro figures on the Pinocchio float were taken from a float in the previous daytime parade, Celebrate a Dream Come True.

Epcot

Pavilion Logos
Fences near the security check at the entrance to Epcot include designs that were used to represent individual EPCOT Center pavilions, or to refer to the park itself.

Pet Care Kennel
One white building to the side of Epcot's main gate was a kennel. Until the Best Friends Pet Care facility opened in 2010, every theme park had its own pet kennel near the front entrance so that animals brought on vacation could be kept with the family at the park itself, and could be visited at various points during the day if the visitors stepped outside the main gate to see them. Most of the facilities were converted for backstage use after the Best Friends Pet Care facility opened to centralize kennel operations.

Presidents on Spaceship Earth
Numerous Audio-Animatronics figures in Spaceship Earth are duplicates of U.S. Presidents used elsewhere at Walt Disney World. In Spaceship Earth, the characters are either unknowns or unfamiliar faces, and faces "borrowed" from historical figures were perfectly acceptable. Because Spaceship Earth called for so many Audio-Animatronics figures, it was deemed simpler to make use of the molds in place for the numerous figures created for the Magic Kingdom's Hall of Presidents. William Taft is the Egyptian priest, and Zachary Taylor is a Roman solider while Teddy Roosevelt is the Roman senator. Franklin Pierce and John Tyler are

Islamic scholars, and across the way, John Adams is the writing monk. James Buchanan portrays Gutenberg, Dwight Eisenhower plays the lute, and Ulysses S. Grant appears as a sculptor. Several figures in Spaceship Earth also come from the American Adventure. Look for Chief Joseph as the cave shaman, the Depression-era store owner as the Phoenician seafarer, Andrew Carnegie at the printing press, the banjo player as the steam press operator, and Matthew Brady as the telegraph operator.

Carousel of Progress Characters

The minstrels off to the right side of the Renaissance set of Spaceship Earth are duplicates of the father and daughter characters in Carousel of Progress in a further example of saving money by re-using Audio-Animatronics figures in more than one location.

WDI on Spaceship Earth

The park design arm of the company, Walt Disney Imagineering, is famous for leaving behind subtle nods to itself. On Spaceship Earth, this once took the form of a radio booth microphone bearing the initials WED, as though that were the name of a radio station. But WED (short for Walter Elias Disney) was the name of the park design division that would later be renamed as Walt Disney Imagineering. A 2008 revision to Spaceship Earth altered the microphone's tribute to instead say WDI.

Original Theme of Spaceship Earth

Most of the vignettes in Spaceship Earth revolve around communication, especially written communication. The storyline, originally developed with the aid of science-fiction writer Ray Bradbury, traces a continuing metaphor of writing on walls that eventually graduates into portable, and then digital, communications. An upgrade to the attraction in 2007 morphed the theme somewhat, especially in the sets near the end of the attraction, away from communication and toward technology in general, which was a better match for new sponsor Siemens. A lengthy scene involving communication across the World Wide Web was replaced with a historical look at room-sized computers and then the garage-based birth of the personal computer.

WorldKey Video Restaurant Reservations

Adjacent to Guest Relations, a curved wall with boarded windows is all that remains of a video restaurant reservation system called WorldKey. Patrons would step up to one of the video monitors to discover a live feed of a reservation attendant, who could also see and hear the patrons via a camera mounted nearby, and the reservations were made just by having a conversation. Essentially video conferencing, the system wasn't more efficient than a face to face reservations counter would have been, but it did have an air of futurism. The location next to Guest Relations was the second home for WorldKey, which was originally situated at the exit to Spaceship Earth.

Energy Logo

One part of the tile mural at the doorway to Ellen's Energy Adventure is a remnant of the pavilion's original design. Each pavilion in EPCOT Center originally had its own stylized logo that was prominently displayed on maps, signs, and at the attractions themselves. Over time, most of those logos have disappeared, but this one is remains at the entrance to the attraction.

Universe of Energy

One line of the narrator's monologue in Ellen's Energy Adventure pays tribute to the attraction which preceded it. As our theater vehicles pull into the last room to hear the Final Jeopardy answers, the disembodied Jeopardy narrator waxes poetic about energy: "Energy: you make the world go around!" This line is a direct quote of the title of a song written by Robert Moline used at the original Universe of Energy pavilion, which featured a celebrity-free variation of the same ride, sets, and movie screens. The original attraction explained the world of energy sources, but without today's humorous narrative storyline.

Riding on Sunshine

The roof of the Energy pavilion is covered with 80,000 photovoltaic cells that generate 75 kilowatts of power, enough power for more than ten residential homes. In the original Universe of Energy, visitors were informed that this solar energy was captured to help power their traveling theater cars, so they had been "riding on sunshine" for the entire show.

Multiplane Animation

The widescreen animation of Earth's formation seen in Ellen's Energy Adventure is a holdover from the original attraction, and historically significant for its use of a multiplane camera to create the illusion of traveling through an animated three dimensional world. Originally invented in the 1930s, the multiplane camera had sat unused at the Disney Studios for over twenty years when it was resurrected for the Energy pavilion. This original multiplane camera later went on display at the One Man's Dream exhibit in Disney's Hollywood Studios.

Horizons

Mission: Space honors its predecessor by displaying the old logo in the gift shop. Housed in a diamond-shaped building where Mission: Space now stands, Horizons offered a ride through sets and movie screens that celebrated futurism, using an "Omnimover" ride system like the one still in use at the Haunted Mansion. The logo for Horizons, a stylized set of straight lines through a central circle, can be seen on the front side of the counter in the gift shop at the attraction's exit. That same logo from Horizons can also be found in today's Mission: Space queue at the center of the enormous gravity wheel. This wheel was a giant set piece from the movie *Mission to Mars* that had to be modified to fit into this building. The X-1 model overhead was also a prop from the movie.

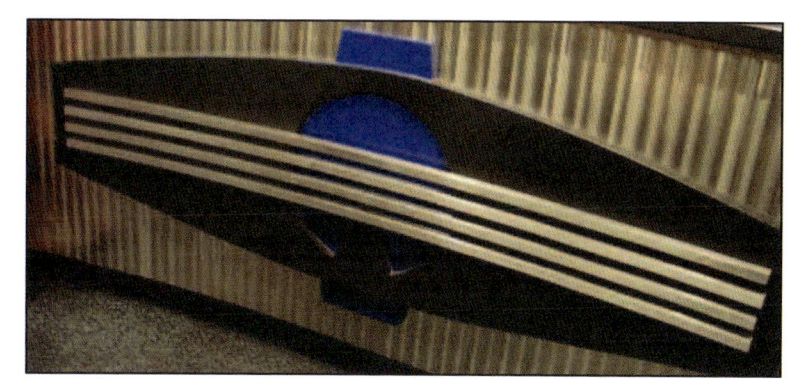

Mission to Mars Crash Landing

A video playing in one monitor at the mission control room of Mission: Space's queue honors the attraction's creative ancestor. The illuminated but deserted mission control room seen at the end of the queue is a tribute all by itself to Mission to Mars, the theme park attraction once found at Disneyland and at the Magic Kingdom. This is the original piece of equipment from Mission to Mars! The homage is made much more explicit by a brief movie clip on one of the console monitors that shows an albatross coming in for a "crash landing." This exact video figured prominently as comic relief in the Mission to Mars control room preshow, but at Mission: Space it only shows every once in a while, as it is part of a much longer loop of other videos. Furthering the inside joke, the onetime host of Mission to Mars, Mr. Johnson, is paged every so often in Mission: Space in that very control room.

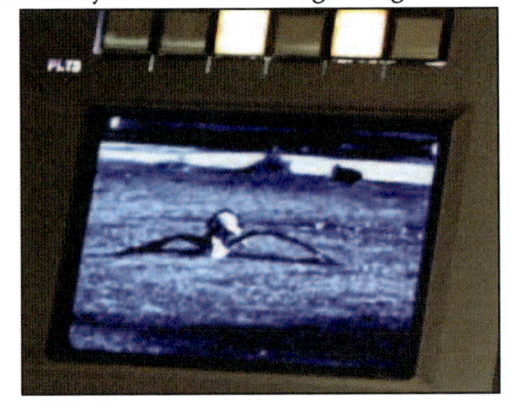

Mr. Johnson from Mission to Mars

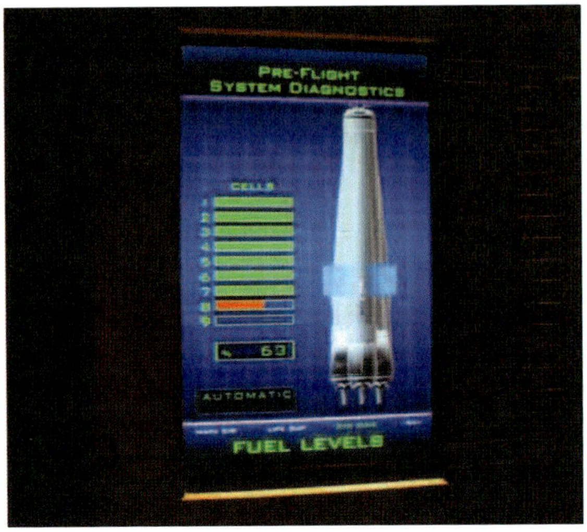

The voiceover at the very last briefing of Mission: Space mentions Mr. Johnson, the former Mission to Mars robotic host: "Attention Mr. Johnson, check the radar, sector M2M." This message is played over the "gantry cam" while visitors are waiting to board, and is usually only heard when there is a significant delay in boarding.

Mission: Space Opening Year

A plaque near the cashier in the gift shop at Mission Space honors the opening year of the attraction. This plaque shows a family posing as astronauts and lists "Epcot 2003," in a rare admission that this is not a true space mission being commemorated, but the theme park ride.

World of Motion Logo

A logo from Epcot's early history is visible throughout Test Track. Before Test Track, EPCOT Center had a ride in the same location called World of Motion (with the same sponsor, General Motors). World of Motion was a slow Omnimover attraction rich with Audio-Animatronics characters, like Spaceship Earth, and had its own pavilion logo. World of Motion is mentioned by name in the window at the entrance to Test Track, and the World of Motion logo can now be seen on trash cans, on a post in the loading zone, and even on the ride itself atop the first hill.

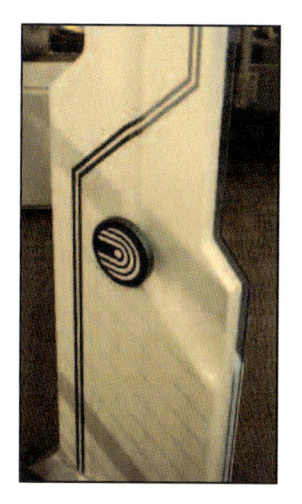

Test Track – First Version

A remnant of the first version of Test Track (1999-2012) can be glimpsed very quickly on the second version of the ride, in the form of a crash test dummy taken from the former queue and now used as the "driver" of the semi truck that almost crashes into us. Crash test dummies were the mascots of the first version of the ride, and we visitors were meant to take the place of such dummies on the track. In the original version of the ride, the ostensible driver of this semi-truck was a flat cutout of President Lyndon B. Johnson, adorned with a Hawaiian shirt and dark glasses.

Fun to be Free

The theme song for Test Track's predecessor, World of Motion, gets a nod on a sign during the ride's thrilling conclusion. Like Test Track, World of Motion was themed around cars, and its slower Omnimover ride system created an opportunity to focus on elaborate sets, Audio-Animatronics, and music. The theme song was "It's Fun to be Free," in acknowledgement of the fundamental nature of automobiles, which make their owners feel free to drive anywhere. This song title can be seen in abbreviated form on a sign during the high-speed finale. There is another sign along this track that memorializes EPCOT Center's opening year of 1982.

The Living Seas

The lifeguard station visible early in the queue for The Seas with Nemo & Friends includes a tribute to the original "Living Seas" pavilion. The original pavilion cultivated the fiction that visitors were taken deep below the surface to an undersea research facility named Seabase Alpha. The lifeguard stand prominently displays the number 5A, an oblique reference to the initials for Seabase Alpha (using a numeral instead of a letter). Nearby in the queue, a sign mentions 1401 Coral Coast Hwy, a reference to the address of Walt Disney Imagineering, at 1401 Flower St. in Glendale. Those seeking hidden characters will note the Hidden Nemo and Hidden Squirt in the cut glass at the end of the loading dock. Others seeking yet more references to the former pavilion must wait for the end of the ride. Mr. Ray's overhead voice at the unload dock exclaims "Sea Cab knowledge, that's why we explore!"—a reference to the original "sea cab" vehicles that traversed the fish tank, though without additional theming. In the second floor observation deck of the main aquarium, glance overhead to spot now-dormant monitors, which used to provide information about the types of fish before us, back when the focus of the pavilion was more about education than entertainment. Lastly, the pavilion's original commemoration plaque still hangs on a wall near the exit door.

Imagineer Fulton Burley

A casual reference in the sea cab voiceover at The Seas With Nemo & Friends honors a longtime Disney voice actor. In the voiceover, we hear mention of Commander Fulton, a reference to voice actor Fulton Burley, the voice of Michael in the Tiki Room. He worked a total of 25 years at Disneyland's Golden Horseshoe Revue, alongside Wally Boag (also present in the Tiki Room as José). Fulton Burley enjoys numerous tributes at Walt Disney World. In addition to the reference at the Seas with Nemo & Friends, his name appears at Fulton's General Store in Port Orleans Riverside, and again at Downtown Disney, in the lessee-operated restaurant Fulton's Crab House.

The Living Seas Sea Cabs

The corridor visible along the bottom of the big aquarium of The Seas with Nemo & Friends contains the "EAC" portion of the ride, but also preserves a remnant of the former attraction here. Before it became The Seas with Nemo & Friends, this pavilion was host to a more scientific-oriented celebration and exploration of liquid space, and it boasted a much more modest Omnimover ride past the same picture windows into the big aquarium. Because there was no East Australian Current to watch in the long tube, passengers simply looked to windows on either side, as well as some directly overhead. While those windows cannot be seen from inside the tube now, they can still clearly be seen from the upstairs observation post after exiting the ride. Television monitors in that observation deck are also leftovers from the educational element of the pavilion in its former incarnation.

Turtle Talk With Crush

A wall-sized screen in one corner of the Seas with Nemo & Friends was the former home of Turtle Talk with Crush. When it originally opened, Turtle Talk with Crush was found in the downstairs bay nearest the manatee exhibit, but the lack of a dedicated waiting area made for long lines in the central courtyard of the pavilion. Turtle Talk moved in 2007, three years after its initial opening, to the current location near the ride. When it departed, the main screen once used to display Crush remained behind.

Seabase Alpha

The illusion of the Seabase being on the ocean floor is a carefully cultivated one that can be traced to this pavilion's roots as the Living Seas. As Seabase Alpha on the bottom of the ocean, this pavilion was supposedly deep underwater, and large half-domes in the ceiling of the main area attested to this fact. Inside, projected lights created the illusion of sunlight rippling across the surface of the ocean, ostensibly far above us. This effect dates back to the original Seabase Alpha. A similar effect of water rippling can still be seen in the second floor, just above the waiting area for Turtle Talk.

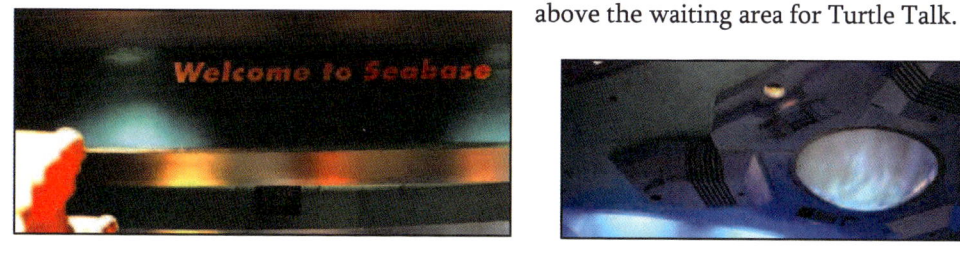

Symbiosis

A plaque outside the Land pavilion refers to symbiosis, the original guiding principle behind the pavilion. All attractions in the original pavilion made reference to the need for a balanced approach to humanity's interaction with nature: they were the Kitchen Kabaret animatronic stage show (balanced nutrition), the Listen to the Land boat ride (balanced approach to farming), and the film actually named *Symbiosis* (balanced relationship with the land). The movie *Circle of Life: An Environmental Fable* (1995) replaced *Symbiosis*, an eighteen-minute video about the complex interrelationship between humans and the earth. Some of the scenes in *Symbiosis* were kept intact for the new movie and can still be seen today. The pavilion's emphasis on the living plants of the planet is obvious, but the pavilion also honors the physical earth and its varied composition via the jumbled tile murals just outside the main doors, meant to capture the layers of the planet's crust. The pavilion's overall shape is meant to evoke a volcano, so it makes sense that we would pass through layers of the planet's crust on our way inside. Elements of the philosophy of symbiosis can still be glimpsed in the décor of the Land pavilion, where colorful balloons in the central courtyard, as well as the name of the nearby food court (Sunshine Seasons), make reference in their markings to the four seasons, as if implying the need for a harmonious relationship with nature through all the seasons. These balloons were originally decorated to symbolize the basic food groups.

Epcot's Opening Year

A subtle sign in Living with the Land honors the year Epcot first opened. The mailbox at the farmhouse has hand-drawn lettering saying "B. Jones 82," a reference to the park's opening in 1982. Then known as EPCOT Center, it was the first theme park opened by Disney which was not a traditional Magic Kingdom, so its turn toward "edutainment" in such attractions as the Land pavilion was a deliberate strategy to imbue the park with an experimental flavor, the better to distinguish it from its Magic Kingdom cousin. Actual trees were used as specific models when creating the molds for the artificial trees in the opening scenes of the boat attraction. The large sycamore outside the farmhouse, for instance, is a duplicate of one standing outside a car wash in Burbank, California—home to the Walt Disney Studios.

Western River Expedition

The mechanized buffalo and prairie dogs in Living with the Land were originally created for a ride in the Magic Kingdom. When the Magic Kingdom first opened, it did not have a long, immersive boat ride with robotic performers. The designers thought there would be no interest in a duplicate of Pirates of the Caribbean from California, since Florida was so close to the real Caribbean. Instead, they designed Western River Expedition, a boat ride through desert buttes and misadventures with all sorts of figures from the Old West. However, visitors asked for Pirates of the Caribbean so often that the Western River Expedition idea was shelved and Pirates of the Caribbean was built instead. The buffalo and prairie dogs, which had already been built, were simply put into storage until they were resurrected at Epcot. Many of the design elements for Western River Expedition ended up being recycled in Big Thunder Mountain Railroad. The Magic Kingdom's version of the ride uses Monument Valley as its stylistic template, which matches the plans for Western River Expedition. In fact, the runaway mine train concept itself started as Thunder Mesa, a mountainous portion of the planned Western River Expedition. The name "Western River" was later used at Tokyo Disneyland, whose river circling their island is called the Western River, and the steam train is labeled the Western River Railroad.

Soarin' Over California

One awkward cut in the preshow video at Soarin' reveals its West Coast origins. Many folks may realize that Soarin' was a transplant from Anaheim's Disney's California Adventure, where it was called Soarin' Over California. The ride showcases only vistas from the Golden State and ends with Disneyland, and the preshow video lists only cities in California. But the host on the video, played by Patrick Warburton, actually mentions the name of the ride: "Hello, and welcome to Soarin'." Visitors paying close attention will realize the actor's mouth shuts unnaturally quickly at the end of this sentence, for this is the result of editing the video and audio away from the original line: "Hello, and welcome to Soarin' Over California."

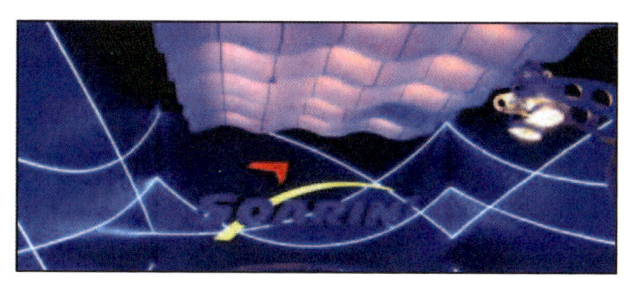

Soarin's Opening Year

Voiceover narration proclaims our flight to be Flight #5505, which is a double reference to Disneyland's opening year (1955) and the first year of Soarin' operation at Epcot, 2005. The ride originally opened at Disney's California Adventure in 2001.

Former Disney CEO Michael Eisner

The attraction features not only one, but two Hidden Mickeys. The more obvious is the mouse symbol made out of fireworks, recalling the effect seen in Disneyland's then-current nightly fireworks, Believe. The less-obvious Mickey can only be seen by those with quick eyes, on the golf ball hit toward the screen. The golfer? None other than then-CEO of the Walt Disney Company, Michael Eisner.

Journey into YOUR Imagination

Originally named "Journey into Imagination," the ride was changed in 1999 to "Journey into YOUR Imagination," with entirely new sets and show elements. Figment and Dreamfinder were ditched as hosts of the traditional dark ride, and new ride vehicles were constructed, with a new ride mechanism. The Figment-free show relied heavily on optical illusions such as a cement block falling through a table, or a fish swimming out of its tank. Some of the optical illusions remain in the attraction today, such as the butterfly in a cage which disappears as we pass by it, or the upside down room, which originally lacked any wild color schemes.

During Figment's absence, he was only represented in the attraction by one clay model in the queue, at the end of the metal shelves. These bits of clay looked unrelated to each other, but when viewed "from the front" they combined to form Figment's familiar head. By 2002, the attraction was renamed again, this time to "Journey Into Imagination With Figment," and many show elements that related to the former hosts were returned to the attraction. The obscure Figment tribute, however, remained in the queue.

Dean Higgins

A doorway sign in the queue for Journey Into Imagination With Figment mentions a fictional character that was in several Disney movies. Higgins was a college dean (played by Joe Flynn) in three movies: *The Computer Wore Tennis Shoes* (1969), *Now You See Him, Now You Don't* (1972), and *The Strongest Man in the World* (1975), a period when Disney tried to weave together an interlaced fictional universe. The thematic connection to *The Computer Wore Tennis Shoes* is especially strong in this attraction. Nearby doors in the queue also honor fictional scientists in Disney movies, such as Wayne Szalinksi (*Honey, I Shrunk the Kids*) and Philip Brainard (*The Absent-Minded Professor*).

The Computer Wore Tennis Shoes

The Imagination attraction incorporates a different tribute as well. An ostensible computer control room for the Imagination Institute pays reference to yet another "mad scientist" movie in Disney's film vault, the 1969 movie *The Computer Wore Tennis Shoes*, featuring Kurt Russell. To honor the movie, the room-sized computer in the Imagination pavilion actually has a pair of shoes at its base, and a letterman jacket from Medford (the college at which the movie takes place) hangs on a nearby peg.

Dreamfinder

A doorway halfway through Journey Into Imagination With Figment offers tribute to Figment's onetime co-host of the attraction. The sets of the current ride were created for Journey into Your Imagination, a Figment-free attraction that was embellished by adding Figment back into it. But Figment got his start in the original Journey into Imagination ride, where he and the Dreamfinder took visitors through bizarre sets to illustrate the variability of imagination and creativity. The Dreamfinder is now referenced just after the Smell Lab, on a door that is labeled "Dean Finder." Sharp-eyed visitors can spot another reference to the Dreamfinder: the cartoon of Figment seen in his upside-down house includes a segment where Figment dresses up in Dreamfinder's distinctive magician-like red hat and cape.

WDI Executives

Small notes posted to a board in the sight lab room of Journey Into Your Imagination With Figment contain insider tributes of various kinds. The note "Tom and Marty -- 5PM" refers to Tom Fitzgerald and Marty Sklar, the top creative executives of WDI at the time. Some of the actual memos sent by the project team during the attraction's refurbishment were also posted in this area.

One Little Spark

The theme song for the original Imagination pavilion is honored in today's attraction. In the climactic scene of the ride, multiple Figment figures are performing various creative activities. Near the center of the set hangs an oversized poster of sheet music for the song "One Little Spark," the theme song of the original version of the ride. An interim update of the attraction that introduced the Imagination Institute without Figment and the Dreamfinder did not play the song, but the modern version of the ride did bring back the melody as an underscore and theme during key moments of the show. The same sheet of music in the finale offers a second nod to the past in the form of a silhouette of the Dream Vehicle—that bulbous contraption that flew through the sky with the aid of a balloon—at the very top of the sheet of music.

A Trip to the Moon

The last set in Journey Into Imagination With Figment makes reference to the former Horizons pavilion. The video of Dr. Nigel Channing (Eric Idle) as the face of the moon recalls a key moment in Horizons, when the Jules Verne story "From the Earth to the Moon" was showcased as one of the visions of the future. In that scene, an animatronic man is catapulted to the moon in a large bullet, and a snippet of George Melies's 1902 adaptation called *A Trip to the Moon* was also visible nearby, in which the moon's entire surface is covered by a face…and the spaceship-bullet lodges itself in one of its eyes.

Figment's Place

For a brief time after Figment's return to the Imagination pavilion, the walkaround Figment character was available for a meet-and-greet in the former Kodak shop between the main pavilion and the theater. Figment's Place is now unlabeled, but the décor inside is still visible through the windows.

Sponsor Kodak

Figment's costume of yellow and red colors is a remnant of the pavilion's original sponsor, Kodak. The initial plans called for a green dragon, but the sponsor Kodak vetoed the suggestion, given that their primary competitor Fuji Film used green prominently in their marketing and packaging. Figment became purple, but the yellow and red colors of Kodak were integrated into his costume. Kodak remained a sponsor of Walt Disney World until the end of 2012.

Magic Journeys

The song "Magic Journeys" from the movie of the same name (which preceded Captain EO as the feature 3D film of the pavilion) can still be heard, in an instrumental version, during the musical loop at the bathrooms of the Imagination pavilion.

Dream Vehicle

A contraption near the ceiling in the gift shop Mouse Gear is a tribute to a prop used in the original Imagination pavilion. Dreamfinder was seen in the original attraction flying through the sky in the "Dream Vehicle," an elongated bulbous vehicle held aloft by an overhead balloon as it traveled through the skies gathering dreams. A smaller replica of the large metallic vehicle used in the attraction is now on display atop a shelf near the ceiling, opposite the cash registers in Mouse Gear. The original Journey Into Imagination was an Omnimover-type ride, with vehicles first circling a round stage that contained the flying Dream Vehicle before entering the larger, more traditional journey through sets that imaginatively explored numbers, letters, painting, and science. The Dream Vehicle was originally intended for an expansion to Disneyland called Discovery Bay. Along with several other futuristic (and yet Jules Verne-esque) vehicles, the balloon-bicycle contraption was meant to be seen along the banks of Rivers of America. The main character of Discovery Bay, Professor Marvel, looked quite a bit in the concept art like the figure who later became the Dreamfinder. Professor Marvel (and by extension, the Dreamfinder) was meant to evoke the Wizard of Oz, and it was no accident that the actor who recorded Dreamfinder's voice for the attraction, Chuck McCann, intentionally tried to mimic the voice of the original Wizard of Oz from the movie, actor Frank Morgan

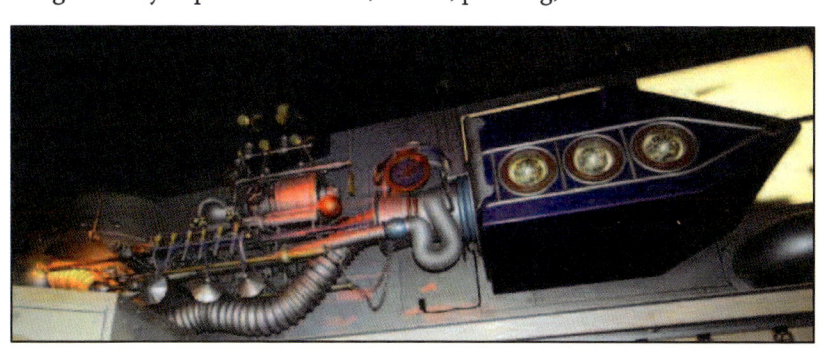

Tomorrowland Steps to Nowhere

Colorful banners outside of Innoventions feature stylized outlines of a staircase, which reflected Imagineer Jason Grandt's obsession as a child with stairs seen from the boarding platform of the PeopleMover, seemingly going nowhere at all. Since Grandt's imagination conjured up an entire hidden attraction one level higher, his preoccupation with the mystery stairs compelled him to mimic their unusual shape when designing the Innoventions banners years later—look for red outlines of vague trapezoid shapes. The DNA letters on the banner spell out "CommuniCore" using DNA codes, as this was the original name of Innoventions.

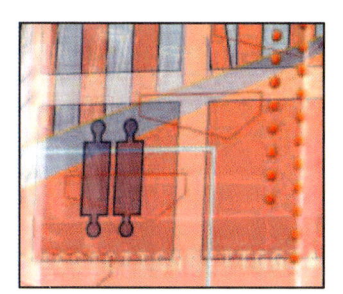

CommuniCore Logo

A sign outside Fountain View honors the park's original designs. As an original pavilion of Future World, CommuniCore (now called Innoventions) had its own logo, which resembled the two semicircles of the building if seen from above. This logo disappeared from use for many years, but reappeared in 2013 as an unobtrusive symbol attached to the back of a Fountain View sign.

Epcot's 25th Anniversary

A seldom-used room in a breezeway of Future World was home to Epcot's celebration of its 25th anniversary in 2007. A colorful timeline of the park's history adorns one wall outside of this room still, though the sign announcing the trinket-filled museum inside no longer appears above the doors. This area had also once been home to Imagineering Labs, where DisneyQuest concepts were tested with the public.

EPCOT Center Logo

In addition to the original pavilions having unique logos, the entire park of EPCOT Center had its own logo, which represented a stylized sphere made up of intersecting ellipses. This symbol is still visible today as an oversized etching in the concrete ground just south of the Fountain of Nations. It can also be glimpsed in the metal security gates outside of the baggage check zone of the main entrance.

Sinkhole

Scaffolding under the walkway bridge near the Odyssey building reveal the girding put in place to prevent everything from falling into a sinkhole. When EPCOT Center was under construction, several monorail pylons were lost to a bottomless sinkhole, and designers realized they needed a way to create a bridge across the water that doesn't depend on pylons. They created a scaffolding system that was anchored to the solid sides of the sinkhole, and to this day the bridge crosses over the void without relying only on direct anchoring in the ground below.

Lights of Winter

Bolts in the ground demonstrate where an illuminated holiday display was located. Until 2009, the walkway connecting Future World to World Showcase was graced during November and December with rows of white arches that played holiday music from loudspeakers overhead. At nighttime, the arches came alive with a multicolored, synchronized light show; the bulbs were made to dance with the music. The Lights of Winter last appeared in 2008. Bolts on the ground on both sides of the walkway, where the arches were affixed each year, are now the only traces remaining.

If You Had Wings

Gran Fiesta Tour honors a former ride in the Magic Kingdom. Several of the interior scenes of the attraction inside the Mexico pavilion, Gran Fiesta Tour, are homages to similar moments from a dark ride in the Magic Kingdom called "If You Had Wings." Examples include the lakeside temple scenes and cliff divers. Even the same songwriter, X Atencio, wrote the theme songs for both attractions. An instrumental version of the theme song from "If You Had Wings" can still be heard at Cosmic Ray's Starlight Café.

El Rio Del Tiempo

Until its 2007 refurbishment, the Gran Fiesta Tour was known as El Rio Del Tiempo, when it offered a more relaxing journey through Mexico, explicitly pointing out the country's history. For that reason, the initial tunnel was framed by paintings of native peoples. These paintings remain in the modern attraction, although the ride is no longer presented as a historically-informed tour, but rather a search for Donald Duck, so that he can perform at a concert that same evening.

Viking Ship Playground

Pieces of the interactive sets used for the Kim Possible cell-phone game were once used as part of a much larger play area built in the shape of a Viking ship. For many years, visitors could clamor aboard a large wooden vessel, which became mere decoration for a while after access was blocked in 2006. The ship was finally removed in early 2009. There were no traditional play area elements left, save for a small see-saw. After the ship was dismantled, the ornate sea-monster mast was retained for use in the Kim Possible Adventure and its successor, the Agent P game.

Rhine River Cruise

A large show building poking out over the embattlements and spires of the Germany pavilion was originally built to house an attraction, a floating journey down the Rhine River. Visitors would have witnessed scenes from the Ruhr valley, picturesque Heidelberg, the moody Black Forest, and the festive Oktoberfest. The entrance to this attraction would have been through an oversized archway now home to a large painted mural.

Never-Built Epcot Pavilions

Remnants of a once-planned Africa pavilion remain between the China and Germany pavilions. The minimal theming done here was simultaneously a test of color and thematic matching with its surroundings and an attempt to entice some African governments to sponsor a pavilion at Epcot. When sponsorship never materialized, the area became a minor shopping and refreshment area. Other planned exhibits include one dedicated to Russia, with enormous onion domes and a ride, and one for Switzerland, which would have brought a version of Disneyland's Matterhorn roller-coaster to Epcot. Partnerships were also explored with Spain, Israel, and Venezuela. In all cases, the lack of sufficient sponsorship spelled the end to the projects.

Good Beats

One thatched hut in the unheralded African section of World Showcase still advertises its old line of business. Now used to display hand-carved trinkets, this hut bears a sign atop it proclaiming "Mdundo Kibanda," which is Swahili for "Good Beats." The name makes no sense now, but its meaning snaps into focus if you know that the first occupant of this space used to sell drums instead.

Imagineer Rick Rothschild

Designers of the American Adventure attraction left behind images of themselves. The original show director for the American Adventure, Rick Rothschild, can be found in the attraction's lobby as a silhouette portrait just to the right of the entrance door, though a phony ponytail has been added to his profile. The other silhouette portraits are other Imagineers who worked on the project. They had these silhouettes created at the Magic Kingdom's Main Street store.

Imagineers at Thanksgiving

The painting of a Thanksgiving scene on display in the second floor of the American Adventure lobby, just before entering the theater, was painted by Imagineer Sam McKim to include numerous personalities from Imagineering and his own life. For example, fellow Imagineer Harriet Burns was the model for the mother in the painting, and the boy with the dog is none other than Sam's son Brian.

Imagineer Blaine Gibson

The farmer statue on the side of the American Adventure was modeled after Imagineer Blaine Gibson's own father (who had been a farmer in the Great Depression). Gibson's first draft showed a more serious farmer in dire straits—it was the Depression, after all—but that was deemed too negative for the show. That gave Gibson the chance to take creative license with his father's likeness and create a happier version; this was his father as Gibson himself had always wanted to see his dad, but never could in real life.

Imagineer Randy Bright

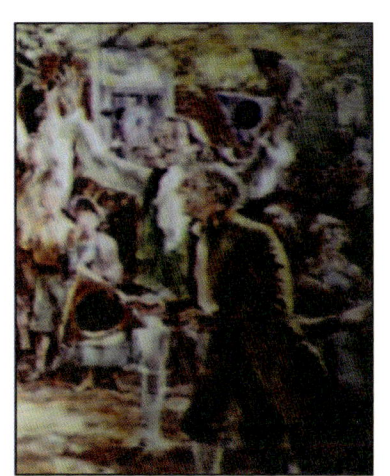

Another Imagineer luminary can be briefly glimpsed inside the American Adventure attraction itself. Disney Legend Randy Bright appears in the painting of the victory parade as a spectator on the side of the road. As the camera pans out, Bright can be seen with two hands in the air. He had been involved in the creation of this seminal attraction.

Disneyland's Train Station

The "Two Brothers" song in the American Adventure includes a scene filmed at Disneyland. In the film that plays during the song, a train depot is shown, which actually can be found at Disneyland's Frontierland train station. This set of buildings sits opposite the tracks in Anaheim and functions only as decoration.

Imagineer Bob McCarthy

The father figure in the Two Brothers segment of the American Adventure was played by Imagineer Bob McCarthy, the man then in charge of Illusioneering, the team in WDI which focused on creating illusions in the theme park environment. The two brothers themselves are Imagineers John Olson and Jeff Burke. They were used as photo models for the Two Brothers slideshow, and the Audio-Animatronics characters created to match the slides used the Imagineers' likenesses as well.

American Adventure's Third Narrator

The American Adventure show was originally conceived to have three narrators, each one spanning a century of American history. For this reason, Ben Franklin symbolizes the 1700s and Mark Twain the 1800s, but there is no third narrator for the 1900s. Originally, the third narrator was meant to be Will Rogers, but designers realized three was a crowd when it came to narrating the show, and the decision was reached to leave the century unrepresented by a host.

Meet the World and Mt. Fuji

A large show building behind the Japan pavilion was once slated to receive Meet the World, a show like the American Adventure, and was later considered for the base for a thrill ride to take place on Mt. Fuji. The ornate castle covers most of the building, but it can be glimpsed looming over the other buildings.

Renault Product Placement

Two flags appearing suddenly at the corners of the *Impressions de France* movie are there to mask a former sponsor of the attraction. Originally, Renault sponsored the attraction and had a prominent product placement appear on the side of the film. When the sponsorship ended, a waving flag was substituted for this entire screen to block out the no-longer-sponsor, and a second flag was added on the other side for symmetry. A similar approach was used in the Timekeeper movie, when Jules Verne zipped around a modern racetrack, and the former sponsor Renault had to be similarly covered up.

France's Film Crew

Members of the film crew on *Impressions de France* are visible in the finished movie as a group on a bicycle ride, who were allowed to be in the finished product as a perk. The director is also part of the show; he is visible with his wife on a cruise of the river Seine viewing Paris from the water.

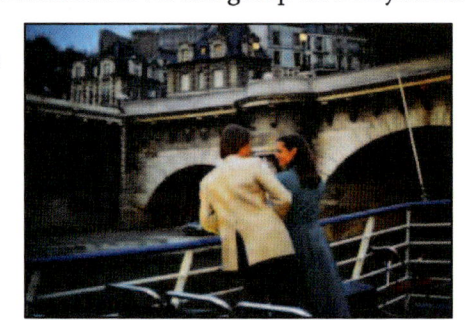

La Signature

The sign for La Signature in the France pavilion is a holdover from a previous shop now out of business. The second story of the perfume shop can be seen today from the ground floor, but the staircase is roped off and inaccessible. Originally, this narrow upstairs gallery was used to display authentic celebrity signatures for sale to the public. Since the prices were high, however, there were few takers and the store closed permanently.

Chefs de France

The names of the three "chefs of France" who contributed to the Epcot restaurant Chefs de France can be seen just outside the entrance to Monsieur Paul. The three names, Paul Bocuse, Gaston LaNotre, and Roger Verge, are on separate signs outside the main door of Monsieur Paul, whose name is itself a tribute to Paul Bocuse. Until 2012, this upstairs restaurant was known as Bistro de Paris.

Mary Poppins Buildings

The building at the back of the pavilion facing the garden was constructed using blueprints for a building found in the film *Mary Poppins*. Buildings in the United Kingdom pavilion represent different centuries in its history, from the 1500s to the 1800s.

Totem Poles

The Mill Stage outside the Canada pavilion was once used as a working mill; it was in this structure that totem pole artist David Boxley created the totem poles now visible in the Canada pavilion.

Disney's Hollywood Studios

Sights & Sounds

A marquee on Keystone Clothiers owes its unique shape to a former attraction that operated here for only a year when the park opened in 1989. Called Sights & Sounds, it allowed visitors to create their own music videos (and take them home). The phrase "You oughta be in pictures" now occupies the spot where the store's name was once visible.

Cover Story

The name of this store on Hollywood Blvd. is a remnant of its original mission, which was to snap photos of park patrons and put their images onto magazine covers (which could be purchased for a nominal fee). The "cover story" was the Guests themselves. Although the store is now a more traditional shop with varied merchandise, its name is a remnant of the time when it had a more singular purpose.

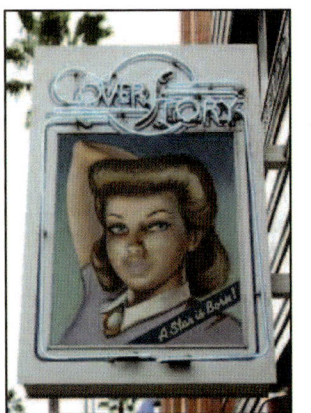

Hollywood Designers

A shop on Hollywood Blvd is named to give recognition to famous Hollywood fashion designers. The "Adrian and Edith's Head to Toe" shop can trace its name to Adrian Greenberg and Edith Head, two famous costumers from the heyday of filmmaking. Adrian was also mentioned in *Golden Dreams*, a now-removed film that was an opening-day attraction in Disney's California Adventure, as the creator of the ruby slippers from *Wizard of Oz*.

Disney-MGM Studios Logo
The dedication plaque for Disney's Hollywood Studios, located at the end of Hollywood Blvd at the foot of a statue of a filmmaker, not only mentions Disney-MGM Studios by name, but displays the logo as well. The park changed its name in 2008.

Anaheim Produce
The Anaheim Produce stand lives up to its name by selling fruits, but its moniker is also meant as a nod to Disneyland Park, which is located in Anaheim. A sign across the back says "Between Palm and Katella," which is roughly the location of Disneyland (at one time, that part of Harbor Blvd in Anaheim was known as Palm).

Imagineer Diego Parris
The billboard atop Sunset Blvd showing a cameraman filming a cereal commercial pays tribute to a veteran Imagineer. Diego Parris, the WDI liaison for television tapings, was placed into the sign as the cameraman, in a nod to his normal role for the company.

Tower of Terror Movie
The collection of suitcases on the sidewalk of Sunset Blvd make reference to the 1997 movie *Tower of Terror*. The suitcases are far up the road from the eponymous attraction, much closer to Hollywood Blvd than the tower, and are labeled with the names of their owners. These names, such as Carolyn Crosson or Gilbert London, are characters from the movie.

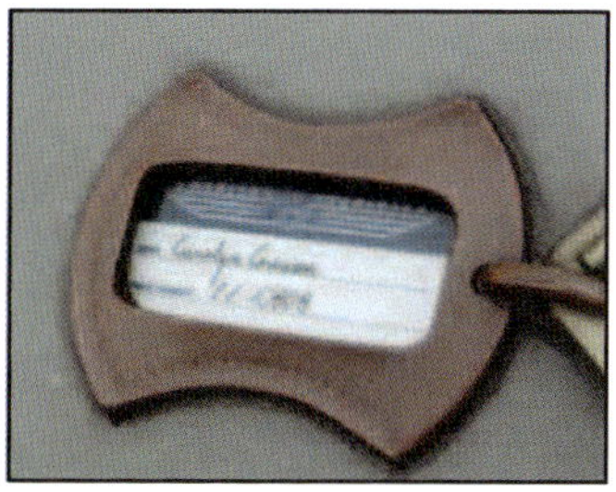

Carthay Circle Theater
One shop on Sunset Boulevard replicates the theater which originally premiered *Snow White and the Seven Dwarfs*. The Once Upon a Time store halfway down the street is reminiscent of the Carthay Circle Theater. That theater in Hollywood held the world premiere in 1937 of *Snow White and the Seven Dwarfs*, and was also the location of the 1929 premiere for the first Silly Symphony, *Skeleton Dance*. A mural inside the Hollywood & Vine restaurant prominently features the Carthay Circle Theater, with *Snow White and the Seven Dwarfs* listed as the marquee film. Other recreations of famous landmarks in Hollywood include the Chinese theater and the Brown Derby restaurant, but almost every structure on Sunset Boulevard and Hollywood Boulevard in the park is modeled on real architecture from greater Los Angeles, not all of it famous.

Snow White Premiere

An audio snippet running infrequently in the background music at the Once Upon a Time shop pays homage to the premiere of Disney's first animated feature, *Snow White and the Seven Dwarfs*. This shop in Disney's Hollywood Studios was deliberately constructed as a tribute to that seminal moment in the company's history. The background music stops for a few moments every hour to play an excerpt of the radio coverage of the premiere. Additionally, photographs around the shop capture the night of the premiere and Hollywood celebrities in all their finery.

Sunset Blvd Expansion

The date of the park expansion to include Sunset Blvd. and its attractions, June 1994, is commemorated on the red trolley merchandise cart visible on the street. This trolley bears the number 694 (as in 6/94) as its production number. Additionally, a shop on the street is conveniently named Ninety-Four for the same reason.

Disney's War Effort

Insignia and artwork found at Rosie's All-American Café come from actual art created by the Walt Disney Studios during World War II. Because so many of Walt's animators were called to duty, the studio had to shut down normal production and made war films and patriotic cartoons rather than feature animated movies for a while. Over 1,000 custom insignia for Allied military units were created by a special team within the studios.

Mortimer Mouse

Contractor stamps in the sidewalk of Sunset Boulevard pay respect to Mickey Mouse's original name, Mortimer Mouse. The stamps say "Mortimer & Co. Contractors, 1928"—the same year that Walt Disney lost creative control of Oswald the Lucky Rabbit and created Mickey Mouse instead. A plaque at the FASTPASS machines for Tower of Terror likewise refers to 1928, in this case as the founding date for Sunset Hills Estates. Other references to 1928 can be seen atop the building at the corner of Hollywood and Sunset and above the restaurant named "Hollywood and Vine." These and many other dates found nearby reinforce the area's theme as Hollywood set in the late 1920s and early 1930s.

The Twilight Zone

The Tower of Terror includes several references to the television show that inspired its theme, *The Twilight Zone*. Dozens of references scattered around the attraction pay tribute to various episodes of the famous black and white show. In the library, visitors can see a small red machine that answers yes or no questions and a book called *To Serve Man*, both items from the television show. Inside the elevator, an inspection certificate is numbered 10259—a reference to the very first airing of the show on October 2, 1959. After the drop, the basement contains still more references to the show, such as a slot machine and a ventriloquist's dummy.

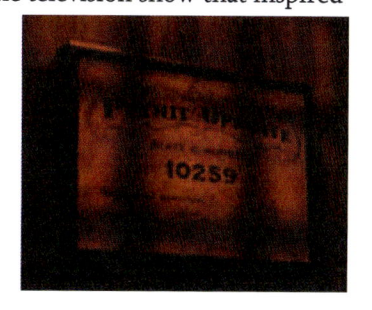

Black Les Paul

There's a remnant from the early days of the ride in the video preshow for Rock 'n' Roller Coaster. During the pre-recorded video, Aerosmith guitarist Joe Perry looks out into the audience as the band is preparing to leave and says "Hey Chris, can you grab my black Les Paul?" These days, the line has no obvious reference because nothing happens as a result, but originally, a Cast Member standing with the audience would nod at the command, pick up a black Les Paul guitar from the ground, and leave the room. The bit of interaction was meant to lend authenticity to the video, as if the band were really on the other side of the glass. The name Chris was chosen to allow for both men and women to play the role.

Imagineering Phone Number

The phone number for Walt Disney Imagineering hides in plain sight in the queue for Rock 'n' Roller Coaster. A sign on the chain link fence in the final queue and boarding area displays: "Buena Vista Fence Co – 544-6500 – Serving you since 1952." Buena Vista is a well-known name associated with Disney (due to an early version of the studios being located on a street by that name). The phone number, in the 818 area code, leads to Walt Disney Imagineering. The final touch comes from the mention of 1952, which was the first year of WDI (then called WED Enterprises).

Rock 'n' Roller Coaster Imagineers

Disney artists and engineers who designed the Rock 'n' Roller Coaster left behind their initials and birthdays on electrical boxes in the queue area, most notably the dispatch console and a box right at the point where the trains launch. The street address for Walt Disney Imagineering in Glendale (1401 Flower St.) adorns one wall near to that launch point, while the nearby chain-link fences include mention of Buena Vista, which is not only the name of an important Disney subsidiary, but also the street on which the Disney studio first began. Imagineers have a long history of granting themselves immortality in their rides, such as the initials that adorn pipes and crates at the Living Seas. Over at the Sci-Fi Dine-In Restaurant, the license plates on each of the cars indicate initials and birthdays of the Imagineers. The mural depicting San Francisco in the Big City area of Disney's Hollywood Studios likewise shows cars with Imagineers' initials on license plates, though one also uses the initials WDI (Walt Disney Imagineering).

8361 Vine Street

A sign for parking, painted in the bricks above Starring Rolls Café, makes mention of 8361 Vine Street, which is an invented address. Vine is a famous street in Hollywood, but to find 8361 you have to travel to nearby Beverly Blvd in West Hollywood, where the occupant is a coffee shop—not unlike Starring Rolls Café.

Brown Derby

The famous Wilshire Brown Derby restaurant in California, originator of the Cobb salad, was notable for an oversize structure in front of the building, shaped like an enormous bowler hat. Later, the Hollywood Brown Derby opened across town, absent the bowler hat. The restaurant at Disney's Hollywood Studios reproduces the Hollywood Brown Derby and thus has no bowler structure out front. Nevertheless, Imagineers paid homage to the bowler hat inside the restaurant, courtesy of a distinctively-shaped light fixture.

Early Animation History

The dinosaur standing in the lake in Disney's Hollywood Studios honors the early history of animation. The world's first animated film debuted in 1914, when Windsor McCay released *Gertie the Dinosaur*, a short film in black and white about a sauropod who displays emotions as she interacts with a lake, a sea monster, and a mammoth. In fact, the film was presented as part of a live vaudeville act; McCay would stand on stage in front of the screen and issue instructions to Gertie that she would appear to act upon; at one moment, he tosses an apple to her and then one appears on screen. Before Gertie and this act, McCay had faced an uphill battle with his audiences, who were inclined to believe that drawings could not come to life. Walt's Laugh-O-Grams and Alice Comedies of the 1920s owed much to McCay's innovations, and when Walt later met McCay's son, Walt stressed how much he owed McCay for his trailblazing.

Dip Site #1138

The Oasis Canteen snack stand took on its present name in 2010, but a corner of its menu sign still pays homage to its former identity. Once known as the Dip Site #1138 (the numbers are a reference to THX1138, the first movie by George Lucas), this stand no longer has overt traces of belonging to the Indiana Jones universe. Yet a sign "behind" the menu implies the entire container is a top secret vessel to be stored in a government warehouse, just like the eventual fate of the Ark of the Covenant in the Indiana Jones movies (and uses the number 9906753, a detail that came from the movie as the crate holding the Ark). The menu on the side of the order window contains the phrase "FIELD TENT #61281" at the bottom, which is a more formal connection to the Indiana Jones universe, as June 21, 1981 was the premiere of *Raiders of the Lost Ark*.

Disney-MGM Imagineers

Mailboxes at the Echo Lake Apartments, between Prime Time Café and Hollywood & Vine restaurant, pay homage to the names of Imagineers who helped build Disney-MGM Studios. Everyone listed on the mailboxes, from John Olson (Field Art Director) to Steve Beyer (Senior Concept Designer) was involved in Disney-MGM Studio's construction. Various job types are represented, encompassing architects, designers, and engineers.

Movie References on Crates

Crates across the lake near the Dockside Diner offer references to famous movies. There's one crate addressed to Rick's Café Americain in *Casablanca*, another to Scarlett O'Hara, one from the Rosebud Sled Company, one earmarked for Max Bialystock, a primary character in *The Producers*, and a final one for George Bailey, the main character from *It's a Wonderful Life*. The name of Min and Bill's Dockside Diner itself is an homage; *Min and Bill* was a 1930 film starring Marie Dressler and Wallace Berry.

Walt Disney's First Office

A sign in the window above Peevy's Polar Pipeline pays tribute to the start of the Walt Disney company in 1923. This sign advertises "Office Space For Rent," a duplicate of the sign seen by Walt Disney on 4651 Kingswell Road in Hollywood, where he found his first office (outside of his garage) in California. Further corroboration comes from the space below. Walt's office had been above the Holly Vermont Realty, and lettering on the door in Disney's Hollywood Studios similarly announces the Holly Vermont Realty.

Superstar Television

The home of the American Idol Experience is the Superstar Television Theater, so named to honor the first occupant of this space. Immediately prior to the 2009 opening of the American Idol Experience, this building was known as the ABC Theater and used for tie-in events with the ABC television network. The original attraction here had been Superstar Television, an interactive show that used audience participants to illustrate television and camera effects. After Superstar Television, it was used for Disney's DOUG Live! and Get Happy with ABC.

Chicken Little Sky

The blue sky painting backdrop on the side of one building (visible behind the Brown Derby restaurant) is a remnant of a promotion in 2005 for the *Chicken Little* movie. Prior to this moment, the Stage 5 building had a normal tan color, but to promote the movie and its "sky is falling" message, the cloudscape was painted here with a missing hexagon. When the promotion ended, the sky was retained as a decoration, though it's now whole without a missing hexagon.

Backlot Tour's Original Entrance

The entryway and queue for the Magic of Disney Animation was once used as the entrance for the Backlot tram tour. Until the Backlot Tour moved down the road to the other side of Mickey Avenue (later renamed Pixar Place), this area and its extensive network of switchback-style queue poles held the hundreds of people waiting to board the trams.

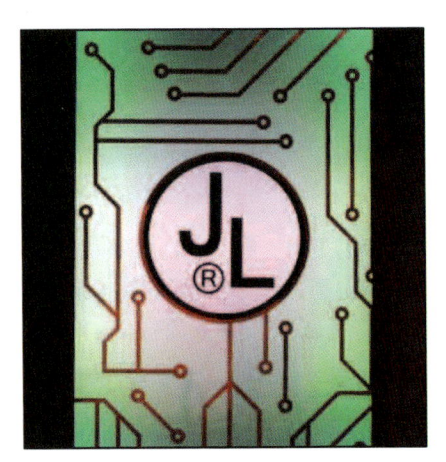

John Lasseter's Initials

The longtime creative chief of PIXAR (and later the entire Disney animation unit) John Lasseter is honored in the meet-and-greet area for Wreck-It-Ralph. Several illuminated signs of a circuit board bear his initials, as though JL was the name of a company. In fact, it appears nearly identical to the logo for Underwriters Laboratories, a safety testing and certification company.

Animators at Work

One of the defining features of Disney-MGM Studios was its status as more than a theme park; it was also a working production studio. Accordingly, a highlight of the Magic of Disney Animation building was witnessing animators at work, bent over their desks. The large glass windows used for this viewing remain in the Disney Animation building and form the back wall of a post-show lobby just after the first movie in the attraction. Now tinted to hide the other side, this glass was once transparent and viewers could watch movies such as *Mulan* being created, one cel at a time.

Nine Old Men

Handprints in a central courtyard at Disney Animation come from several of Walt's "Nine Old Men," longtime animators that proved their worth across many projects and decades. Walt's term of endearment is in reference to the "Nine Old Men" traditionally said to populate the Supreme Court. These handprints and signatures were inscribed by the animators themselves during the park's opening in 1989. The names include Marc Davis, Ken Anderson, Ken O'Connor, Ward Kimball, Ollie Johnston, and Frank Thomas.

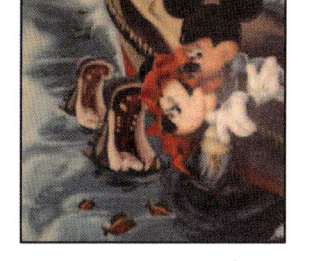

Anaheim's Piranhas

The Jungle Cruise poster at the Magic of Disney Animation references the Disneyland version of the ride. The Meet Minnie attraction is stuffed full of inside jokes, one of which highlights the famous boat ride in Adventureland. The Trader Sam in the corner is modeled after the one found in Anaheim, however, rather than the one visible in Orlando. And the piranhas jumping out of the water can only be found at Disneyland, not the Magic Kingdom. The date across the top of the poster seals the tribute, as it mentions July 17, the opening date of Disneyland in 1955. This poster also mentions Imagineering legends and executives such as Patrick Brennan, John Lasseter, Harper Goff, Bill Evans, and Marc Davis.

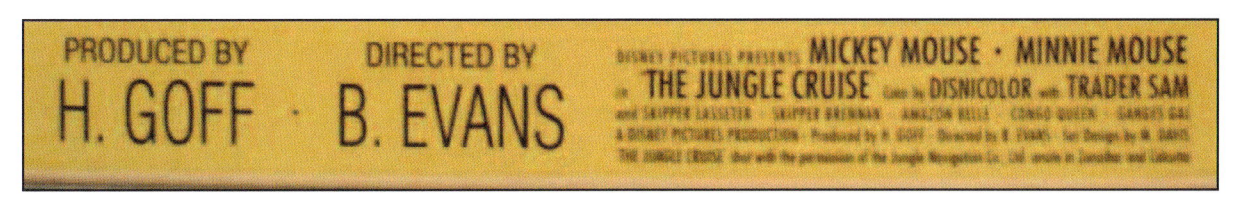

Disney Afternoon Shows

Posters in the Meet Minnie queue also mention characters from the Disney Afternoon, a line-up of cartoons that ran in the afternoons in the 1990s. The Mary Poppins poster mentions Kent Powers, a character from *Quack Pack*. You'll also find mention in various places of Drake Mallard (the other identity of Darkwing Duck), Fenton Crackshell (*DuckTales*), and Webigail Vanderquack (*DuckTales*).

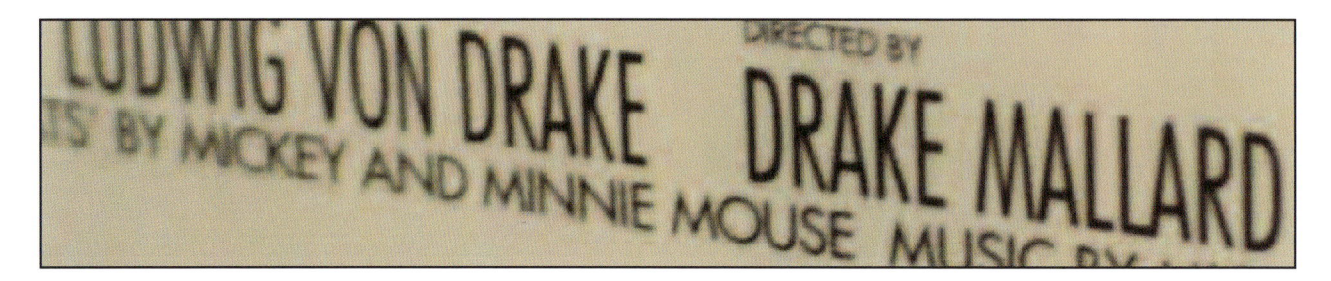

Harrison Hightower

One poster in Meet Minnie makes reference to a character invented for Tokyo DisneySea. The "Bride of Frankenollie" poster mentions Harrison Hightower IV, a character invented for the Tower of Terror as seen at TDS, as the screenwriter for this fictional movie. The same poster functions as a reference to animators Frank Thomas and Ollie Johnston, often seen as a pair (they have a cameo in *The Incredibles* as themselves, for instance).

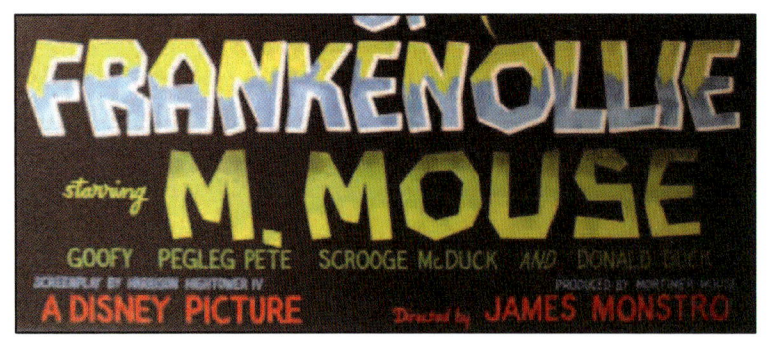

Imagineer Fred Burley

The voice actors behind the Tiki Room birds are honored in the "Mouse Pacific" poster in the Meet Minnie queue. At the bottom of the poster, the credits to "Mouse Pacific" offer doubled references to the Tiki Room, with each emcee bird mentioned as the first name, and the last name of the voice actor given. "Michael Burley" references the bird Michael, voiced by Fred Burley, for instance. The others are "Jose Boag" (Wally Boag), "Fritz Ravenscroft" (Thurl Ravenscroft), and "Pierre Newton" (Ernie Newton). In the background of "Mouse Pacific" poster can be seen the Tiki Room as it appears in the Magic Kingdom. Near the Tiki Room image is a bird in flight; this is the Orange Bird, the original sponsor of the area when it was called Tropical Serenade. Apparently eager to include as many references as possible, Imagineers also made mention on this same poster of the famous Sherman brothers who composed many songs, including the Tiki Room's main anthem.

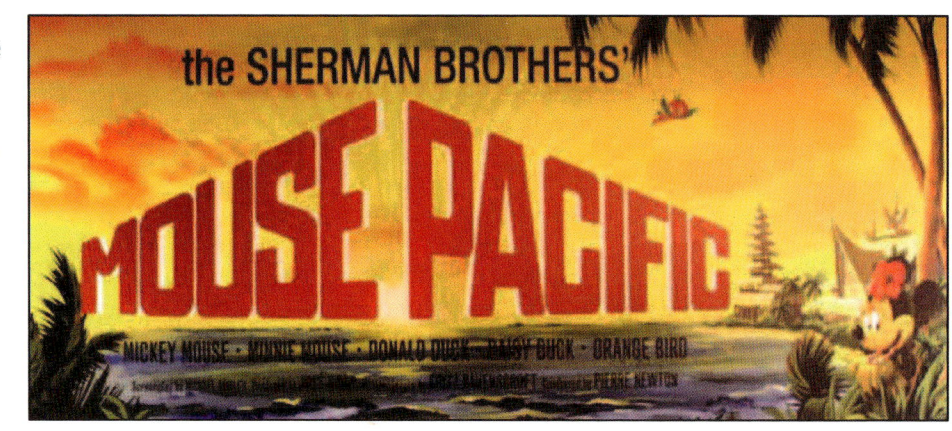

Mortimer Mouse and Oswald

The Cleopatra poster is "presented" by Mortimer Mouse, Walt's name for his new creation that his wife Lillian renamed to Mickey. Walt had needed a new character after Oswald the Lucky Rabbit was taken from him via a contract loophole, and Mickey (originally named Mortimer) was born on a train back from that fateful meeting where Walt learned of his loss of Oswald. The Oswald connection is not forgotten, however, as his name appears on a couple of posters as well. The Mortimer Mouse shown near the Oswald art was an early graphical concept for what became Mickey Mouse.

Muppet Monorail

The moving rock prop that propels Ariel around the stage in Voyage of the Little Mermaid is a leftover machine from the previous show in this space, Here Come the Muppets. In the original show, the Muppets crash "onto" the stage via a monorail. The machinery used to achieve the effect was preserved for the Little Mermaid show, and re-dressed to look like a rocky outcropping.

Hollywood Agent William Morris

One yellowed "wanted" poster on the right side of the Great Movie Ride vehicle, near the top of the pile of such posters in the Western set, references Hollywood talent agency William Morris. The poster is one of many that promises a reward for an arrest concerning a robbery of Wells Fargo, and it's offered by "Wm B. Morris, Agent." When the Tiki Room was rethemed to be "Under New Management," the two barker birds out front were named William and Morris in a similar nod to the mega-agency.

Glendale Galaxy

One of the screens in the *Alien* scene of the Great Movie Ride makes mention of Glendale, the home city for Disney Imagineers. This monitor can be seen at ground level, on the left side of the ride vehicle, and includes other jokes about the goo seen dripping in the attraction.

```
THE NOSTROMO WELCOMES ALL ALIENS VISITING TODAY FROM THE
GLENDALE GALAXY.  WE HOPE YOU HAVE A PLEASANT STAY WITH US.

GOO VISCOSITY: VERY GOOEY / REMARKS: EEEEOOOOO  / ENGINEER: G. KOCH
TIME TO NEXT SPECIAL EFFECT FAILURE.......45.8 YEARS
```

Aliens Tribute

The Great Movie Ride also folds in numerous witticisms in the small print not often read closely. This is most noticeable in the spaceship Nostromo, the section dedicated to the movie *Alien*, where a floor-level monitor off to the left side uses very small typeface to list names of people involved with the movie as well as tongue-in-cheek references to Walt Disney World itself:

- Eric Jacobson - System Alteration Supervisor
- Bob Joslin - Unexplainable Phenomenon Expert
- Glenn Koch - Intergalactic Goo Analyst
- Bob Weis - Spaceship Driver
- Kathy Rogers - Coordination Coordinator
- Brock Thoman - Outer Space Planner
- Doug Esselstrom - Shirt Supervising Officer
- Geoff Puckett - Video Eyewash Designer
- Jack Gillett - Re-Wiring Specialist
- Walt Steel - Technical System Untangler
- Doug Griffith - Still Programming the Witch
- Craig Russell - Everywhere at Once
- John Sullivan - Looking for Ron Beumer
- Tim Kirk - Interior Detail Expert
- Mike Vale - Ear Damage Officer
- Michael Sprout - Operation Manual Re-Writer
- Carol Rotundo - Star Search Astrophysicist.
- Listed as ** MISSING ** are Eric Swapp, Robin Reardon, Cory Sewelson, Ron Beumer, and Paul Osterhaut.

Pharaoh Mickey

Decorative hieroglyphs hidden in the wall of the Great Movie Ride honor Mickey Mouse and Donald Duck. Mickey, dressed as a Pharaoh, is being served food by Donald, shown as a slave, in a stone carving in the Indiana Jones room of the Great Movie Ride, opposite the scene where the Ark of the Covenant is being opened. Set slightly above visitors' heads, this block is seldom noticed unless sought directly. It can be seen to the left of the ride vehicle, after passing the second Anubis statue and in the corner of the room, about halfway up the wall.

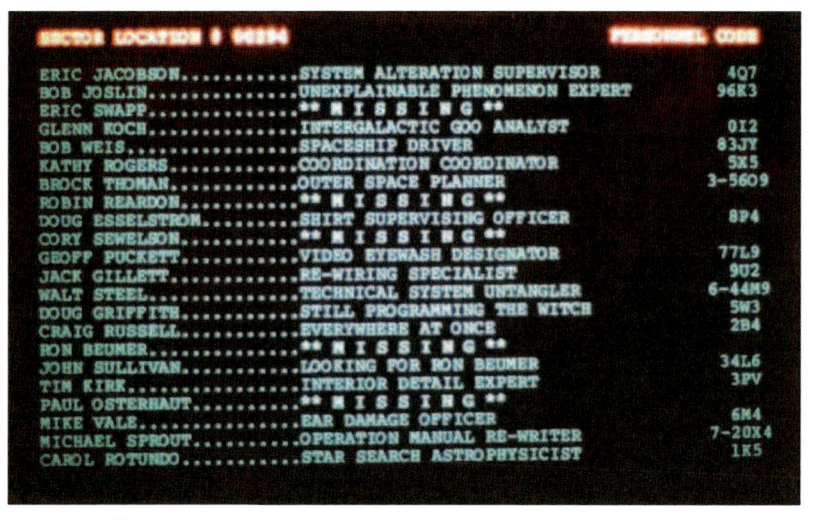

Hieroglyphic Droids

Part of the decorations elsewhere in the same room is a tribute to R2-D2 and C3PO, the droid partnership from the Star Wars movies. C3PO especially is drawn as a stylized figure a bit like hieroglyphics, rather than a more direct representation like Mickey and Donald. The connection with Indiana Jones is a fairly direct one, since George Lucas was the creative force behind both franchises. The hieroglyphic droids can be found at eye level, in the middle of the room on the left side.

Tarzan as a Pirate

The swinging Tarzan in the Great Movie Ride was duplicated for Disneyland Paris. When building the French version of Pirates of the Caribbean, designers wanted to inject additional excitement into the attraction in the form of sets and elements not found in the American versions of the ride. One such innovation was a pirate swinging from a rope right over the boat full of Guests. The Tarzan figure from the Great Movie Ride provided a ready-made mold for the Paris attraction; they merely had to change the costume and duplicate the figure.

Casablanca Plane

The plane in the background of the *Casablanca* set of the Great Movie Ride is not from the movie, yet has its own interesting tale. Persistent urban legend claims that the plane used in this set comes from the movie *Casablanca*, but there is conclusive evidence that no real plane was used in shooting that scene, and they used a mock-up instead that was smaller in scale. Disney purchased a full-sized, real Lockheed plane for the Great Movie Ride. The back half of the Disney's Lockheed was put to use elsewhere in the property, in the Magic Kingdom's Jungle Cruise. This prop can be seen near the animatronic of the elephant and the African savannah.

Wizard of Oz Tornado

The fans and swirling visuals during the Sorcerer Mickey portion of the Great Movie Ride were originally created to approximate being inside a tornado, meant as an introduction to the Wizard of Oz set that followed. The transition to a crashed house, complete with crushed witch below, would have been complete if this section were themed to the tornado, but contract negotiations with MGM dictated that the Wizard of Oz sequence not last three sets, but only two. As a result, the already-built first set was repurposed for the Sorcerer's Apprentice scene.

Radio Disney

When Disney's Hollywood Studios (then Disney-MGM Studios) first opened in 1989, it held working production facilities and soundstages, not just to simulate but actually to be a working studio. As part of this effort, Disney's then-new radio network called Radio Disney was given production space next to Sounds Dangerous. While signs on the windows remain (now proclaiming WDW Radio Studio), the facility has been vacant for some years.

Walt Disney World Opening Year

The first year of Walt Disney World's existence – 1971 – is honored yet again in props outside the entrance to the Indiana Jones Epic Stunt Spectacular. Near a trunk labeled with H. Jones's name are several artifacts. One cup is tagged as though for storage with a large "71", facing the sidewalk. There are no accidental mentions of 71 in Walt Disney World!

Indiana Jones Movie Props

Life-sized vehicle props at the exit to the Indiana Jones Epic Stunt Spectacular were taken from the third movie, *Indiana Jones and the Last Crusade*. The flat bed truck and the distinctive tank, while appearing now in a state of advanced decrepitude after a long stint exposed to the elements, are the same vehicles used in the filming of the movie.

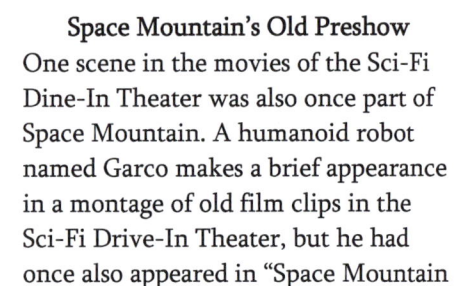

Space Mountain's Old Preshow

One scene in the movies of the Sci-Fi Dine-In Theater was also once part of Space Mountain. A humanoid robot named Garco makes a brief appearance in a montage of old film clips in the Sci-Fi Drive-In Theater, but he had once also appeared in "Space Mountain TV," a video in the queue of Space Mountain that showed ostensible channel-surfing through FedEx commercials and whimsical news shows. There identified as Galactic President Garco, he actually traces his lineage on film to a 1957 episode of the show "Disneyland," on an episode called "Mars and Beyond" that postulated life on Mars. That queue video at Space Mountain was rife with references to old Disney properties. One could glimpse the ship from Flight of the Navigator, visible when Crazy Larry tried to sell used spaceships. Crazy Larry was himself famous in Disney circles: the actor was Charles Fleischer, voice of Roger Rabbit. There was a Hidden Mickey in the form of a satellite unfurling radio antenna ears, as well as a tribute to the old ride Mission to Mars, in the form of a downward view of a rocket launching that was once part of the attraction.

George Lucas

One verbal terminal announcement pages Egroeg Sacul (George Lucas spelled backwards), a holdover announcement from the ride's previous incarnation.

Tom Morrow

Another verbal announcement mentions Mot Worrom (Tom Morrow backwards), which honors an Audio-Animatronics figure from Tomorrowland's past (at Disneyland, there was actually more than one such figure!)

Starship Enterprise

Decorative "plates" on the wall opposite the Starspeeder in the Star Tours queue make mixed reference to both *Star Trek* and *Star Wars*. The *Star Wars* references include the upper part of one plate, which says 2R-OP3C (backward for C3PO and R2), while the middle of the second plate which says IG0088, in reference to a robotic bounty hunter with that name from *Empire Strikes Back*. The *Star Trek* references are also scattered across both plates. One plate displays the code N1C7C01, which is the Enterprise call sign (NCC-1701) with the numbers mixed into every second letter. The middle part of the other plate, meanwhile, shows JK0966, a reference to Captain James Kirk and the first month of the *Star Trek* broadcast in September 1966.

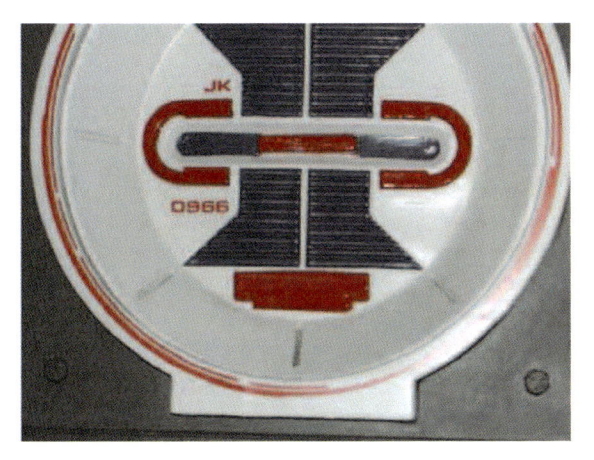

Imagineer Tony Baxter

In the corner just below (just after) the overhead screen, look for lettering in dim light saying TWB3000. This is in honor of Senior Vice President of Creative Development at WDI Tony Wayne Baxter, who was one of the driving forces to get the first Star Tours made at Disneyland, and the old Star Tours flight number 3000.

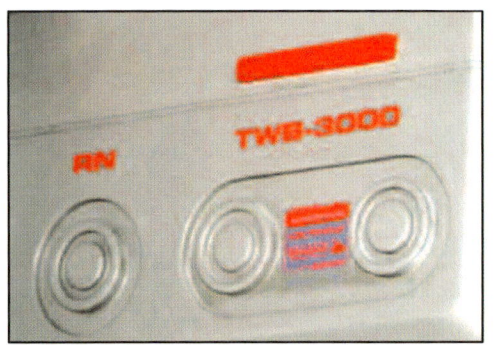

Los Angeles Area Code

One stenciled code on the queue walls in Star Tours refers to the telephone area code in Los Angeles, where much of the Walt Disney Company is headquartered. The code reads 21B3ABY, which is barely scrambled for "213, Baby!" as if a Los Angeles resident wanted to enthusiastically tout his area code (213).

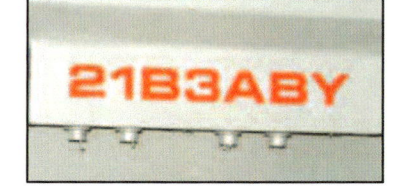

WED to WDI

The dedication plaque on the outside of the Starspeeder, written in Aurebesh, uses large letters to include "WED" on the left side and "WDI" on the right side of a red-colored arc. WED was the original name of the division now called Walt Disney Imagineering.

Imagineering Street Address

Every trip on Star Tours ostensibly takes place on Flight 1401, as heard in the dialogue on the ride itself. This is one of many references to Walt Disney Imagineering, which is located at 1401 Flower St in Glendale, CA. The Starspeeder in the queue is thus labeled with 1401 in several places.

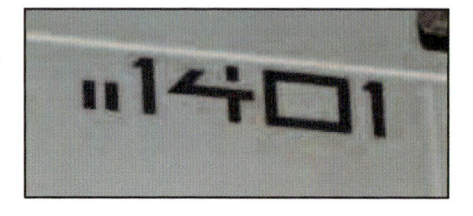

Captain Rex

As you cross into the second queue room, look to your left to spot Rex, our pilot in the original version of Star Tours. He's now marked "defective" and is being sent back for repairs. Listen for a while and you'll hear some audio from the original ride.

TK-421

The Stormtrooper who "wasn't at his post" in the original Star Wars movie is honored here with a sign just above Rex and the other droids. Note that TK421 is again referenced by the luggage droid, who sees a stormtrooper helmet in the scanner and wonders why he's not at his post. The remaining numbers, 731*81, are not as easily explained, but could be a birthday (7/31/81) of a contributing Imagineer.

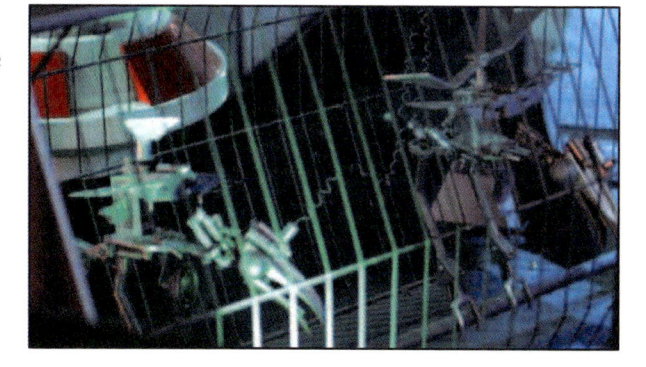

Robot Birds

In the original Orlando queue, robotic birds sat atop the entry door just after the second G2 droid—they looked a bit like Salacious Crumb, the lackey "monkey" near Jabba in the movies. They are now encased in a cage near Rex, no longer animated.

Star Wars Movie Dates

A sign in the Star Tours queue recognizes the source material for this attraction by listing all the dates of the *Star Wars* movies. The long string of painted numbers and letters, below a pipe and near a noticeable sign saying "Droid Customs," includes the two-letter years for the release of all the films, including *Star Wars: The Clone Wars*: 77, 80, 83, 99, 02, 05, and 08.

America Sings

The two droids in the second queue room were remodeled slightly in the rehab, but you can still see their webbed feet and wagging tails – these animatronics began life as oversized geese in America Sings (later the Innoventions building) in Anaheim's Tomorrowland. You can see identical geese – their brethren – who were later moved from American Sings to the first indoor scene of Splash Mountain in Anaheim. The whole thing was reproduced from scratch in Orlando, so the "history" is referential rather than direct.

Imagineer Tom Fitzgerald

The voice of G2-9T, the G2 droid who is working the luggage scanner, belongs to Tom Fitzgerald, a senior executive with Walt Disney Imagineering. Tom had also recorded the voice for G2-9T in the original Star Tours—in his words, "because there was no one else there to do it"—when he was an Imagineer earlier in his career, so it made sense to bring him back as the voice of the same droid for the refurbished attraction.

Opening Date of Star Tours

Star Tours in Anaheim opened on January 9, 1987, so any mention of 109.87 is no accident. This number appears on the front side of the "suitcase tube" behind G2-9T. Even though this attraction is in Orlando, it pays tribute to the original version of the ride in California.

Luggage Jokes

There are 71 different bags scanned in the Star Tours queue, with 71 a further reference to the 1971 opening date of Walt Disney World. Not all seventy-one scans offer a tribute or inside joke, but many do:

- Battle droids who say "you can call me Roger, if you want to" (a *Bambi* reference)
- Major Domo from Captain EO
- Buzz Lightyear toy, who says "To Tatooine…and beyond!"
- Captain Rex
- *Incredibles* suit
- Space helmets labeled with logos for Space Mountain and DASA (Disneyland Aeronautical and Space Administration) from Disneyland in the 1970s
- G2-9T sings "Star Tours, nothing but Star Tours"—a tribute to a "Star Wars" parody song created by SNL's Bill Murray  
- Wall-E
- V.I.N.CENT from *Black Hole*
- Figment
- Sorcerer Mickey hat and broom
- Wall-E's Christmas lights, VHS tape, and shoe with plant in it
- Bear trap, which G2-9T gleefully identifies: "It's a trap!"
- R2-D2 mouse ears
- Helmets and discs from *TRON*  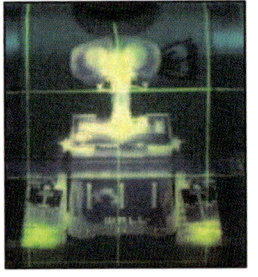
- Monsters Inc. teddy bear
- Everyday items (bee, wand, key, etc) that sound out "Obi Wan Kenobi" when spoken aloud
- Indiana Jones's whip and fedora
- Goofy doll
- Chip and Dale
- Madame Leota crystal ball
- TK-421's stormtrooper suit
- A Goofy hat (said by G2-9T to look like Jar Jar Binks)
- Microscope and snowflakes to honor Adventure Thru Inner Space, the dark ride that was replaced by Star Tours at Disneyland
- Aladdin's lamp
- Luke's set of mouse ears

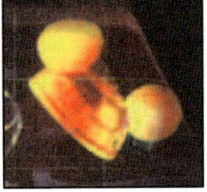

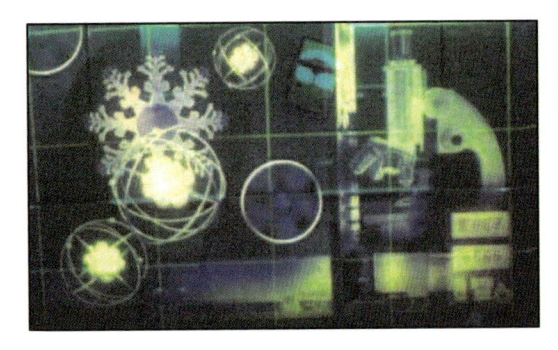

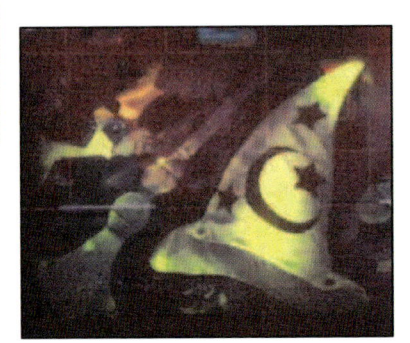

Verbal References

G2-9T at one point berates the audience "You just think about that!" in the same tone of voice used by Ellen DeGeneres in Ellen's Energy Adventure, who chides us "You think about that next time!" at the end of the preshow, when talking about leaving car doors unlocked. This is not the only time G2-9T makes a verbal inside joke. When discussing his life as a scanner, G2-9T says "this job is a lot better than, say, fixing broken droids all day" – which was his job prior to the refurbishment (and he even sang "I've been working on the same droid / all my livelong day"). Finally, when talking to himself, G2-9T remarks that it's a "boring conversation anyway," echoing language used by Han Solo on the Death Star intercom while breaking Leia out of the detention center.

Hidden Mickey R2 Droid

The shadow figures at the bend in the upramp include an R2 unit with Mickey ears (also known as R2-MK, when appearing at the Star Wars Weekends in Disney's Hollywood Studios).

Frozen Jar Jar

Another shadow figure at the bend in the upramp is a representation of Jar Jar Binks encased in carbonite. This is a nod to the vocal detractors of the Gungan character who openly called for his demise in the movies.

K-DROID

In the original Star Tours queue in Anaheim, a radio sat opposite G2-9T on the first upramp, displaying "107.9" (it was different in Orlando) with the announcer calling it K-DROID every few moments. In the new queue, when on the second half of the upramp, look down at G2-9T to spot a panel labeled KDRD 107.9.

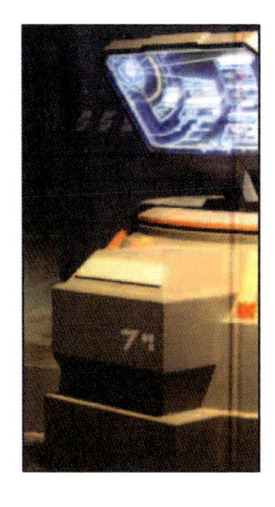

WDW Opening Year

The ever-popular reference to 1971, the first year of Walt Disney World's operation, can again be seen in Star Tours. The last Audio-Animatronics figure in the queue, a robot on our left voiced by Patrick Warburton, stands atop a pedestal. Look to the base of this pedestal to spot the stylized "71" on the sides.

Soarin'

The second droid is voiced by Disney veteran (and Soarin' host) Patrick Warburton. This droid quotes the Soarin' safety video with phrases like "place all carry-ons in the overhead comPARTments" and "nice work, pal."

Delta Airlines

A prominent safety spiel on Delta airlines uses a coy tone of voice and wagging finger to say "smoking is never allowed on Delta flights," and Ali San San uses much the same phrase about smoking and photography in a clear homage. The original Delta video was filmed by Katherine Lee, who was nicknamed "Deltalina" by online fans or her distinctive finger wag. Ali San San's name is meant as a subtle reference to the first name of actress Alison Janney, since she gave voice to Ali San San.

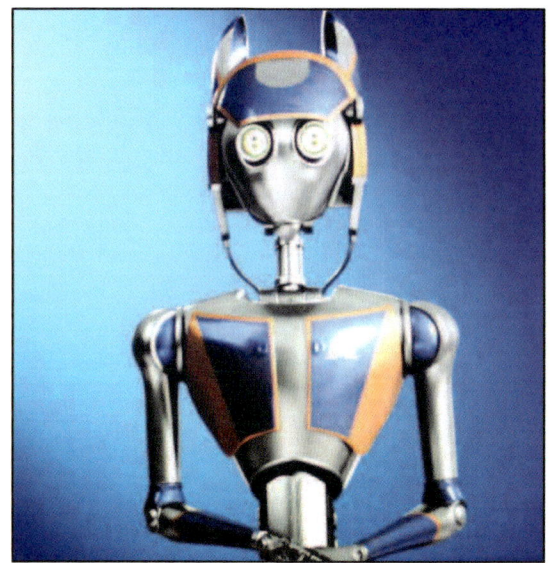

Dex's Diner

Ali San San was created using a computer-generated model taken directly from *Star Wars Episode II: Attack of the Clones*, where it was the waitress in Dex's Diner. This saved money since the model did not have to be created from scratch again. A similar trick was used with the signal droid guiding our Starspeeder in the attraction's film; this droid was once a window-washer in the films.

Imagineer Jenny Mulholland

The woman who demonstrates how to latch a seatbelt in the safety video for Star Tours is the same person who appeared in that role for the original version of the safety movie—Imagineer Jenny Mulholland. She was featured on the Tokyo Disneyland version of the queue video, as well.

Star Tours Original Phrases

Many phrases from the old version of Star Tours are used almost exactly in the new version. One example: "Star Tours – What are you doing here? This is a combat zone. It's restricted. Ease off on your main thruster" was a phrase in the old version; it is largely kept in the new movie during the Hoth scene: "Star Tours – This is a restricted area. What are you doing here? Stay clear of the combat zone." A second such echo occurs in the podracing scene. In the original movie, Rex claims "I've always wanted to do this! We're going in!" when diving into the Death Star trench. In the new movie, C3PO says something similar in Tatooine: "Oh a podrace! I've always wanted to do this!" Threepio elsewhere claims "I have a very bad feeling about that," a phrase from not only the *Star Wars* movies, but also the original Star Tours. Luggage droid G2-9T used to sing "I've been working on the same droid all the live long day!" when he was a repair droid, and now says "I've been looking at the same bag all the live long day!" Finally, in the original movie, Rex screams "Brakes! Brakes! Where are the brakes?!" near the beginning of that version of the attraction. C3PO says the same exact phrase at the end of the Naboo sequence.

Mighty Microscope

A prop honoring a ride displaced by Star Tours can be seen in the asteroids / Planet Mustafar sequence, inside the Death Star. The Mighty Microscope prop is visible on the left side of the screen in the tunnel as we exit the Death Star. The Mighty Microscope was an element in Adventure Thru Inner Space, an Omnimover ride that preceded Star Tours in Anaheim. When Star Tours moved in (1987), the Microscope showed up as a prop in the hangar of the original Star Tours movie (also true of the Orlando attraction, which used the same film).

Imagineer Steve Spiegel

Several insiders are given cameo roles in the Mustafar sequence of Star Tours. This was meant to be the one "winning" episode, where everything goes right for our adventure instead of going wrong. Show producer Steven Spiegel is seen in an orange X-Wing outfit, and visual effects producer Marianne McLean, also from WDI, appears as one of the elders that bows. She's wearing the actual original Mon Mothma costume from the movies. A third WDI person, Frank Reifsnyder, stands on the far back platform, at the very right side of the frame. There are a few extras unrelated to the production, but most of the others in the frame are from Industrial Light and Magic (ILM), the special effects house.

Tomorrowland

In the Coruscant sequence, one of the electronic billboards we fly past includes the "T" logo from Disneyland's re-do of Tomorrowland in 1998, using a rather distinctive font. Also, the word "Tomorrowland" is spelled out in Aurebesh, the *Star Wars* language, on the large display. There are also two Hidden Mickeys in this sequence: the first comes from spotlights in the city in the lower-right corner of the frame, and the second from ventilation shafts along the back wall after our speeder lands and descends into a cargo bay.

Horizons Mold

A mold for a vehicle once used at Epcot's Horizons can be seen at the Backlot Express restaurant. Atop one corner of the dining area in this restaurant is the mold used to create a hovercraft used in Horizons, the original pavilion to occupy the spot now taken by Mission: Space. Horizons celebrated the "future that never was," with often quirky visions of the future which never came to pass. The hovercraft was located in the foreground of a scene where oranges were being harvested by remote-controlled vehicles. A robotic butler sporting many arms was another iconic scene from Horizons that manages to resurface as part of a video every so often somewhere in the Disney park empire. Disneyland's Innoventions flashes an image of the robotic butler, for instance, as did the "One Man's Dream" movie that Disneyland opened in its Opera House to celebrate its Golden Anniversary in 2005.

Walt's Subway
The subway lines, listed as supposedly running below the Big City/Streets of America façades, honor Walt Disney by using "W" and "D" as the names of the subway lines. This part of the set is meant to represent New York, which like many cities around the world uses letters for subway routes.

A113
The classroom A113 at Cal-Arts was home to many future artists and directors during their studies, and it has appeared as an inside joke in all Pixar movies. A reference to it appears on the Streets of America, in the window display for a travel agency. Specifically, the ticket clutched by Donald includes the A113 designation.

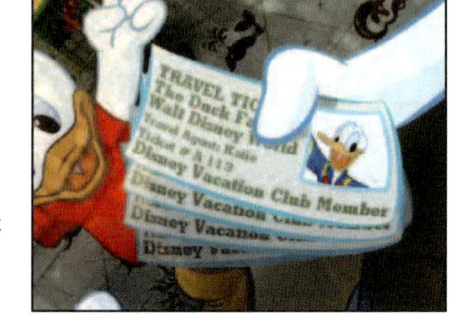

STOLport
A trophy in a window display case honors Walt Disney World's little-seen runway. The mini-airport for Walt Disney World, a Short Take Off and Landing (STOL) strip, still sits to the side of the parking booths at the entrance to the Transportation and Ticket Center, but hasn't been used for aviation in decades. A trophy in a display case celebrating cars on the Streets of America mentions the STOLport as well as L.B.V. (Lake Buena Vista).

Toad Car
Another trophy in the same display case presents a replica of the cars used on Mr. Toad's Wild Ride at the Magic Kingdom. This display case is full of other tributes, such as the mention of "Bill Pete" (in reference to Disney artist Bill Peet) and the more correctly-spelled "Peet's" cans next to the brand labeled "Holloway," in reference to Winnie the Pooh voice actor Sterling Holloway. Look near the top of the display for a mention of WED, the early name for Walt Disney Imagineering.

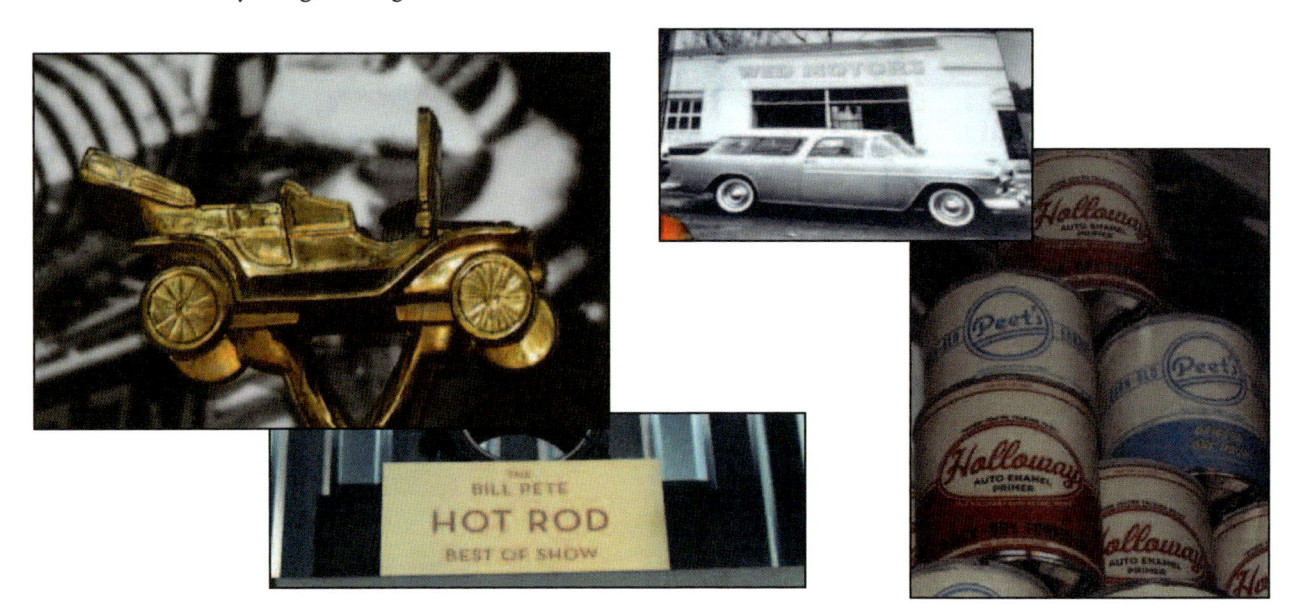

Jennings Osborne

An illuminated outline of a razorback pig at the Osborne Family Spectacle of Dancing Lights is a tribute to the family patriarch who started their tradition of massive displays of holiday lights. When Jennings Osborne died in 2011, the display that year at Walt Disney World added a new razorback pig in recognition of his favorite football team from the University of Arkansas. In fact, it's Arkansas, not Florida, marked in that spinning globe in the sky! Other Osborne family tributes can be found in the form of electronic stockings with the names of all family members, and a unique cat in the display, which was part of the Osborne family's Halloween decorations that accidentally made the journey to Walt Disney World in 1995, and it's been included ever since (forming a favorite "find the cat" game for return visitors). Osborne was willing to move the display to Walt Disney World since he had lost an Arkansas State Supreme Court case in which his neighbors forced him to turn off his over the top show in his own neighborhood. Besides, the nativity scene had been purchased at Epcot's Italy pavilion in the first place!

Dan Summers

A cast member nametag on the illuminated toy soldiers in the Osborne Family Spectacle of Dancing Lights honors the man who worked on the display in an integral way. Dan Summers, a technician on the team who installed the lights each year, figured out how to make them dance to music. When he died in 2009 of cancer, a nametag in his honor was installed on the central toy soldier (the one with the mouse ears).

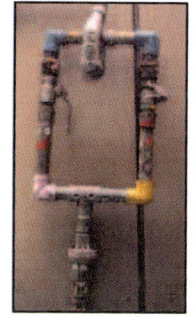

NBC Pipes

Painted pipes in the alleyway queue next to MuppetVision pay tribute to plumbing in a closet famously painted by Jim Henson and Franz Oz. While waiting for their segment of the Jack Paar program to be filmed, the performers discovered a closet with pipes in their dressing room, and filled the time by painting whimsical features on the pipes. The NBC Pipes, as they came to be known, eventually became part of their studio tour.

MuppetVision Marching Soldiers

A few of the marching soldiers that appear in MuppetVision 3-D can be seen in the ceiling of the preshow area. The preshow is home to numerous inside jokes, such as the spaceship Swine Trek used in "Pigs in Space," a picture of Muppet creator Jim Henson, and even a Hidden Bunsen Honeydew and Beaker (represented as a ball with glasses and a whistle with bulging eyes). Inside the theater itself are further gags, such as the sheet music in front of the penguin orchestra—it's the music for "The Rainbow Connection," a song that appeared in the first Muppet Movie. In typical Muppet style, there are also puns and wordplays scattered about the attraction. The preshow sports a net full of jello (spoken aloud, it sounds like Annette Funicello), as well as a crate labeled 2-D Fruities (i.e., "tutti frutties"). The projector inside the auditorium is labeled as a Yell & Howell model, which is simultaneously a play on words ("yell and howl") and a reference to a prominent manufacturer of projectors named Bell and Howell.

Muppet Movie Props

Set pieces reproduced in the Stage One Company Store, a shop near MuppetVision, include the lobby of Happiness Hotel (from *The Great Muppet Caper*) and the lockers doubling as micro-apartments (from *The Muppets Take Manhattan*). Look up high for cutout flats of a bus and a delivery truck, from the Muppet-produced musical "Manhattan Melodies", part of *The Muppets Take Manhattan*.

Here Come the Muppets

Static Muppet figures of Dr. Teeth and the Electric Mayhem near the ceiling in the Stage One Company Store are from a former show at the park called "Here Come the Muppets." Located in the theater later used for Voyage of the Little Mermaid, Here Come the Muppets was a live puppetry show of the gang talking to Mickey Mouse by phone, and later joined by other Muppets who crash a monorail onto the set.

Toy Story Parade

Little green aliens hanging in the ceiling at Pizza Planet are remnants of the Toy Story Parade, which ran in Disney-MGM Studios from 1995 to 1998, when it was replaced by the Mulan Parade. These props would bob their heads slightly as the floats moved, and hints of their free-motion necks can still be glimpsed if you examine them closely in the ceiling.

Star of the Day

Photographs in the lobby of Mama Melrose are remnants of a program from the first months of the park's existence. Called "Star of the Day," the program brought actual celebrities to the park, one per day, so that visitors could feel like they were in the real Hollywood and could glimpse an actor and get a signed photo. The program was discontinued by the second year, and leftover prints from those collections were used to decorate Mama Melrose.

Roger Rabbit Ride

The building at the exit to Backlot Tour was so themed because this area was once slated to receive a *Who Framed Roger Rabbit* makeover. Due to this connection, the term ACME is used several times in this store. In that cartoon universe, ACME is considered a generic but ubiquitous name. The Roger Rabbit expansion was once set for the end of Sunset Boulevard and would have included a ride on flight simulators called Toontown Trolley, a dark ride called Baby Herman's Runaway Baby Buggy Ride, and Benny the Cab, the dark ride that later became Roger Rabbit's CarToon Spin at Disneyland. This expansion of "Roger Rabbit's Hollywood" was to have been part of the "Disney Decade" of expansion at the theme parks, which would have included a land behind Main Street in Disneyland, Westcot duplicating Epcot in Anaheim, and a Beauty and the Beast dark ride at the Magic Kingdom. Creative differences between Disney and the other respective owners of the Roger Rabbit property meant development never got off the ground, and only the warehouse remained. There is also a glass window near Echo Lake that recalls a scene in which Roger crashes through a window leaving only his outline behind. Another nearby sign in Echo Lake advertises Eddie Valiant, his co-star. A further reference to Roger Rabbit can be found in the Backlot Express restaurant dining area, where visitors can climb aboard the stripped-down chassis of the vehicle that was used to film sequence for Benny the Cab. Some sort of vehicle platform had to be physically present to hold the live-action actors, but because most of the car was later animated over the filmed portion, it lacks a roof and sides.

Mermaid Statue

The statue of a mermaid near the Backlot Tour is a prop from the movie *Splash* (1984), but it has other equally interesting stories to tell. For instance, the figures of the fountain were created originally for the movie *Herbie Goes Bananas* (1980). The statue is ideal to place here, since the movie *Splash* spawned a sequel named *Splash Too* (1988), which was the first movie to be filmed at Disney-MGM Studios. This tribute is one of the few at Walt Disney World to actually be acknowledged with a plaque explaining the history.

Main Street Antiques

While some of the movie props in the warehouse are highly recognizable, such as the rocket backpack from *The Rocketeer* and the taxi cab used in *The Great Muppet Caper*, most of the artifacts appear unremarkable. Yet several are recycled objects from Walt Disney World's history; hitching posts and antique mutoscopes transported from the Magic Kingdom's Main Street welcome visitors to the warehouse, for instance, and banners used in World of Motion adorn one wall.

Disney-MGM Studios Park Map

Memos, park maps, and other letters in a display case at the entrance to the Backlot Tour warehouse display the old name (Disney-MGM Studios) and logo of the park, which changed in 2008 to Disney's Hollywood Studios.

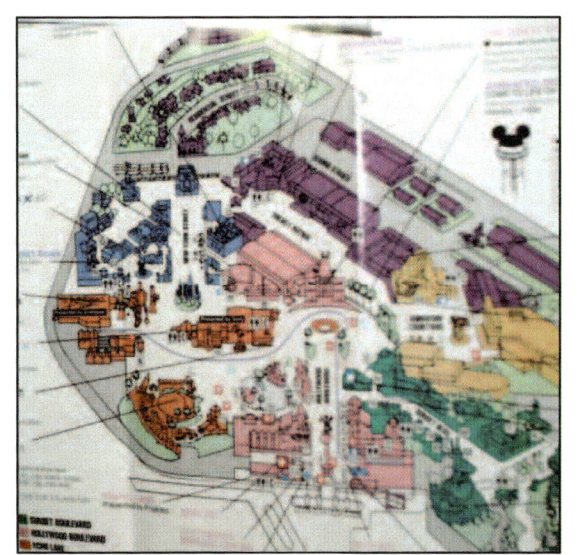

World of Motion Props

Some of the props in the warehouse at the Backlot Tour came from the former attraction World of Motion. The warehouse is used as a queue for visitors waiting to board the trams, and it is crammed full of props used in movies, as well as several artifacts from Epcot's former ride World of Motion, which celebrated the history of transportation. Of particular interest are several robotic performers, now unplugged and stripped of their clothing. Examples include a balloonist, a man strapped to a wooden wing, a neighing horse, and a collection of several masks used to give Audio-Animatronics their realistic faces.

The Lottery

A rectangular section of brick wall with a window, seen at the very end of the warehouse in the Backlot Tour, is a remnant of the first incarnation of the Backlot Tour, which took several hours and included a walk-through of several soundstages. This section of wall was used in the filming of "The Lottery," a three-minute movie starring Bette Midler about a winning lottery ticket blowing through the wind. It was the first movie shot entirely at Disney-MGM Studios, which was originally meant to house movie and television production but moved away from that mission over time.

Adventurers Club

An airplane prop and a stone Sphinx on the Backlot Tour, just before the wardrobe drive-through, come from a former nightclub on Pleasure Island. The Adventurers Club was a live-action comedy club, where characters would interact with the public not only while onstage, but while intermingling with the crowd as well. When the clubs on Pleasure Island were discontinued in 2008, these props were moved here.

Disney-MGM Opening Year Vehicle

An antique fire truck on display on the Backlot Tour honors the park's opening year of 1989. Visible along the outside of the wardrobe building, this fire truck announces itself as Engine 89, D.H.S. Fire Co. When the park opened, it had a different name, but this sign honors 1989 without using the old name.

Walt's Airplane

The plane visible on the Backlot Tour is the very one used by Walt Disney to scout the then-undeveloped Walt Disney World property. "Mickey Mouse One," as the plane was called in reference to the presidential plane Air Force One, is a Grumman G-159 Gulfstream I multi-engine propeller plane built in 1963. It was used by Walt Disney and later executives as a corporate aircraft, until it was finally decommissioned in the late 1980s and retired to Disney's Hollywood Studios. While Orlando's main airport saw Mickey Mouse One with regularity, after a while it made sense for Disney to build an airstrip right on Walt Disney World property. Although the idea had been to cater to visitors flying with small commercial airlines from regional airports, Disney's airstrip was never heavily used, as it functioned only as an "uncontrolled" landing strip and could not store many planes. Plans for a Disney-built, wide-winged plane designed for this type of short-takeoff runway (STOLport) never came to fruition, and the airstrip fell into disuse. To this day, the remnants of the airstrip can still be found to the east of the toll booths at the Magic Kingdom's parking lot.

Goosebumps

A themed wall between the AFI Showcase Shop and the Monsters Inc. meet and greet is a remnant from a display for the popular Goosebumps book series. The Goosebumps HorrorLand Fright Show and FunHouse opened in 1997, with the show taking place on the loading dock stage and the funhouse located in the space next door, now occupied by Monsters Inc. characters. The padlocked door was a part of the funhouse theming, and it remained after everything else was removed.

Pixar Director Pete Docter

The director of *Monsters, Inc.* is given a tribute at the meet-and-greet location near the Backlot Tour. Handwritten notes on Walt Disney Entertainment letterhead are signed "Pete D" and remind employees of apparently recent policies, such as to avoid jokes about Jonas since they are "too easy." Jonas is a nod to Pixar employee Jonas Rivera, who was the producer of *Up* (2009).

Looney Bin

The elephant caught in a net, suspended from the ceiling in the Prop Shop (near the exit to Backlot Tour) is a remnant of a Roger Rabbit-themed store in this area. When the park first opened one year after *Who Framed Roger Rabbit* (1988), this store was called the Looney Bin and featured props and decorations from the movie. You can also spot boxes of ACME Eye Balls, which played a role in the movie when they caused Judge Doom to slip and allow our heroes to escape.

Mighty Ducks Mask

High in the rafters of the ACME Warehouse, a shop opposite the Studio Catering Co. restaurant, is an unassuming prop in the form of a white hockey mask, with familiar duck bill. This unique shape is recognizable as the trademark for the Mighty Ducks of Anaheim, the professional hockey team founded by Disney and sold in 2005. Disney had based the name on a 1992 movie, *The Mighty Ducks*. A few years after its sale, the team changed its name simply to the Ducks.

Backstage Pass

Skywalk bridges connecting soundstages in Pixar Place are remnants of the original Backlot Tour. When the park first opened, the tram tour was followed by a walking tour of several soundstages on what is now Pixar Place, and guests transitioned between buildings on the bridges. This part of the tour was later made its own attraction called Backstage Pass, until it closed in 2001 to open up areas of the park to the general flow of visitors.

Luxo Jr. Platform

A brick column with a flat top and no apparent function opposite Toy Story Midway Mania was once home to a performing robotic version of Pixar mascot. The white desk lamp with articulated neck, known as Luxo Jr., was visible to the public for a short while in 2010 as an animatronic figure about three feet high that came from behind this wall and performed on the platform wordlessly. The lamp would express emotions from dejection to delight as different background songs were played, depending on how appropriate each was to the Pixar universe. The figure experienced technical trouble, however, and was not displayed long in the park.

Pixar Corporate Logos

The queue for Toy Story Midway Mania contains two side-by-side references to Pixar. Flanking the Audio-Animatronic Mr. Potato Head barker are the two main symbols of the innovative studio—a ball with a distinctive star pattern can be seen on one side (known as the Luxo ball), while the other side has the desk lamp (named Luxo Jr.) seen bouncing around in the corporate logo before every Pixar movie. The ball is again seen at the end of the ride, visible on one wall just before disembarking.

Toy Story Mania Single Rider Line

The Toy Story Midway Mania marquee retains traces of a single-rider line that was only in use for a few months when the ride was new. Two small, blank rectangular signs near the bottom of the attraction's FASTPASS return sign were installed to cover up the "&" symbol and the words "Single Riders." Originally, single riders were allowed in the FASTPASS return line with no tickets, but this proved unworkable operationally in the long run, and the option was discontinued without major adjustment to the attraction's sign.

Animator Joe Ranft

One blue "book" spine in the FastPass+ queue for Toy Story Midway Mania pays tribute to longtime Pixar animator, Joe Ranft, who died in 2005 in an automobile accident. Ranft is the ostensible author of this blue "book," which is named *Magic Made Easy*, in reference to Ranft's abilities as an amateur magician.

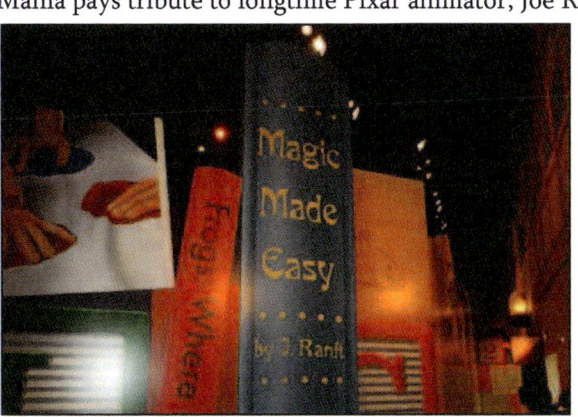

Imagineer John Lasseter

The chief creative officer of Pixar as well as a prominent figure in Walt Disney Imagineering, John Lasseter is often associated with his 1988 short *Tin Toy*, the first completely computer animated short. It comes as no surprise that we see the Golden Books version of this famous story as we exit Toy Story Mania. Sharp-eyed visitors can even spy Lasseter's name, given as the ostensible author of a different green book, seen painted on the wall at the end of the ride. The book Lasseter supposedly wrote? *Tin Toy*, of course. The idea of toys being alive in that story provided Lasseter with the germ of the concept which would later become *Toy Story*, so *Tin Toy*'s presence in the *Toy Story* attraction makes sense.

Granny's Cabin

One of the artifacts in One Man's Dream is the true beginning of the Disney theme park. While there are numerous props and models of significance in this museum to Walt Disney and its special attention paid to theme park history, none approaches the uniqueness of Granny's Cabin. This unique miniature tableau was hand crafted by Walt Disney himself, with help from Ken Anderson and Harper Goff on concepts and designs, to mimic Granny Kincaid's set from the movie *So Dear to My Heart*. Walt's vision was to construct an entire set of such show scenes and display them on a train he'd move around the country (so that poor people would have a chance to see it too), and this idea became known as Disneylandia. The concept would later morph into other location-specific plans and eventually turn into Disneyland in Anaheim.

Dancing Man

The Dancing Man exhibit, also scaled to participate in the roving Disneylandia project, represents a significant leap forward in miniaturized robotics, which was a key ingredient in Walt's plan for a traveling park of miniature show scenes. The robotics and crude 3D animations were what interested Walt the most, and his fascination with them led to the invention of Audio-Animatronics as a key technology in Disney theme parks later on.

Walt's Working Office

This set is not a tribute, but rather an actual remnant of Walt Disney's offices at the studios in Burbank. He had a formal office where he received visitors, and a working office where he actually read scripts and attended to matters on his own. After he died, his offices were extensively photographed and catalogued down to the last detail, then shipped to Disneyland re-created as an exhibit for people to see. His working office was moved to Orlando in 2001 as part of the "100 Years of Magic" celebration, when One Man's Dream was first opened.

Birth of Audio-Animatronics

A small brass birdcage located in Walt Disney's "working" office on display in One Man's Dream was the inspiration for Audio-Animatronics so pivotal to Disney's theme park storytelling. The mechanical bird, purchased in New Orleans, served as the inspiration for the Enchanted Tiki Room's animated birds, the first Audio-Animatronics in Disneyland. This birdcage sat in Walt's formal office when the offices were moved after Walt's death to Disneyland, where it remained for many years. When Walt's "working" office was relocated to Walt Disney World for the "100 Years of Magic" celebration in 2001, the birdcage was transferred to the "working" office and made its way to Florida.

Mary Blair and Walt

One of the newer exhibits in One Man's Dream, installed in 2010, concerns Disney's involvement the 1964 World's Fair and prominently features one of the Audio-Animatronics figures of Mr. Lincoln, as well as the control board for the figure. Behind that is a scale model and concept art for "it's a small world," which also debuted at the fair, and one unmarked photo here shows Walt Disney with doll designer Mary Blair, who was responsible for much of the look of "it's a small world." A nearby sticky note reminds to "check colors," while another one indicates OK with Mary Blair's initials—a logical tribute, since she was well-known for her wild color palettes.

Imagineer Joyce Carlson

The same Mr. Lincoln display also includes a photo of Joyce Carlson, who was the primary designer of "it's a small world" when it was installed at Walt Disney World. Joyce is shown with a Small World doll bearing her likeness, especially the signature glasses.

Imagineer Rolly Crump

A black and white picture amid the Mr. Lincoln display also shows Walt with Imagineer Rolly Crump, who designed the eye-catching "Tower of the Four Winds" marquee display for the 1964-65 World's Fair in New York. Models and drawings of this kinetic sculpture are also visible at the display. Crump later confessed surprise at the appearance of the full-scale exhibit, since he envisioned only slender metal pylons and hadn't anticipated the reinforcing added by the construction engineers.

Imagineer Blaine Gibson

Longtime Disney artist and renowned Imagineering sculptor Blain Gibson is honored at the Mr. Lincoln display as well. Originally an animator who dabbled in sculpting as a hobby, Gibson was recruited into Walt Disney Imagineering (then called WED Enterprises) to design sculptures for such attractions as Great Moments with Mr. Lincoln, Enchanted Tiki Room, Pirates of the Caribbean, Haunted Mansion, and Hall of Presidents. The Mr. Lincoln figure on display represents Gibson's sculpting work, and he is acknowledged via a white lab coat draped over a chair (his embroidered name badge is upside down on the chair, and a WED cap is nearby as a further tribute.

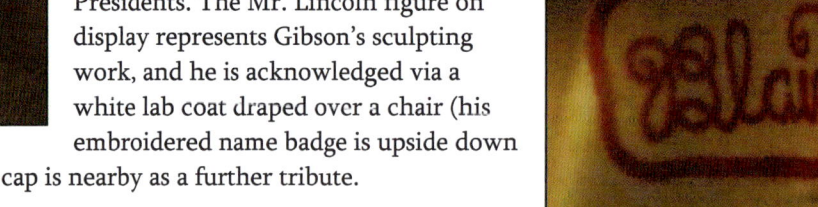

Robot Butler

A full-sized prop from Horizons is on display in One Man's Dream in the form of the robot butler. Horizons had celebrated visions of the future, including many that never came to be, and the robot butler was part of one such Jetsons-type future our society had once envisioned. The same display case also includes one of the Figment Audio-Animatronics from the original Journey into Imagination, a prop Dream Vehicle, and two stuffed animal versions of oversized vegetables from the show Kitchen Kabaret, in the Land pavilion.

Disney's Animal Kingdom

Quest of the Unicorn

One section of the parking lot pays tribute to a never-built attraction in a land that never came to be. The Unicorn section is a nod to Quest of the Unicorn, a planned walk-through maze of mythological creatures, to take place in Beastlie Kingdomme, a land that was never built. Camp Minnie-Mickey was constructed in its place.

Discovery River Boat Tour

Docks on either side of Discovery Island were once used for boats that transported guests around the park's waterways. Originally known as the Discovery River Boat Tour, this attraction suffered long lines and little to look at, so by the end of 1998 it was renamed the Discovery River Taxis, to point out that its function was transportation. That too did not grab the public's attention, and for most of 1999 it was known as the Radio Disney River Cruise, aimed at younger audiences, until it finally closed for good in August 1999. The five boats in the fleet (Crocodile Belle, Darting Dragonfly, Hasty Hippo, Leaping Lizard, and Otter Nonsense) cruised past a few points of interest, like frothy bubbles near Africa meant to imply an underwater creature, or a full-size animated Iguanodon standing in shallow water near Dinoland U.S.A. The boats can sometimes be seen today transporting a live band playing amplified music in the Asia/Dinoland lagoon.

Beastlie Kingdomme

A solitary stone dragon visible from the bridge to Camp Minnie-Mickey honors a onetime idea for a new land.

Beastlie Kingdomme, a land of mythical creatures that never lived, was meant to be built near here in the area once occupied by Camp Minnie-Mickey, and future home of Pandora: the World of AVATAR, but the idea lost out to the need for more children's areas in the park. Land was set aside on the other side of Camp Minnie-Mickey, which was conceived with an Adirondack theme to blend more naturally into the fantasy realm, should that ever be built. When the Discovery River Boat Tour was transporting visitors around the park's waterways, the stone dragon was one of the primary show elements, spewing flames each time a boat came close.

Dragon Logos

Dragon designs on benches throughout the park make reference to Beastlie Kingdomme. Dragons were part of the original plan for expansion of this park right from the beginning. To this day, the official logo for Disney's Animal Kingdom features a dragon silhouette as part of the Tree of Life; this logo can be seen throughout the park on trash cans and other locations. The dedication plaque for Disney's Animal Kingdom, located in the Oasis section of the park, mentions dragons too. Even the ticket booths in front of the park made reference to the original plan to build the park's thematic foundation on the triumvirate of real animals, prehistoric ones, and imaginary ones. A carved representation of an elephant's head adorns the roof of one ticket booth, with a second booth hosting a triceratops, and the third home to a dragon's head.

Jane Goodall's Chimp

A prominent sculpture of a chimpanzee on the Tree of Life owes its existence to biologist Jane Goodall's visit to the park. During construction of Disney's Animal Kingdom, famous researcher Jane Goodall viewed the Tree of Life and wondered why there was no chimp prominently represented. Given a chance to remedy that, she chose David Graybeard, a chimpanzee she had known for a long time, to immortalize near the entrance to It's Tough to be a Bug, and a plaque was placed nearby to explain Graybeard's significance.

Original Kilimanjaro Safari Storyline

A character named Dr. Catherine Jobson in the queue video of Kilimanjaro Safari is a remnant of a different storyline for this attraction from its opening until 2007, when Dr. Jobson's role in the main attraction was removed. Previously, her voice was heard in the safari truck, since she was supposedly traveling overhead by plane with Warden Wilson. She informed the audience of the death of the elephant matriarch Big Red, shot by poachers, and the disappearance of her offspring Little Red. The safari truck helped corner the poachers and recover Little Red. There's an even more direct reference to the storyline via a poster early in the queue, which mentions the animals by name.

Zoo Opening Date

The opening date of Disney's Animal Kingdom is commemorated on a sign at the start of Pangani Forest Exploration. Ostensibly a radio station, ZU2298 doubles as a clear reference to (April) 22, 1998, when the park first opened its doors. In early marketing, park executives wanted to stress that the park was "not a zoo" so marketing materials used the invented word "Nahtezu." Today's radio sign re-uses the zoo/ZU portion of the old tagline.

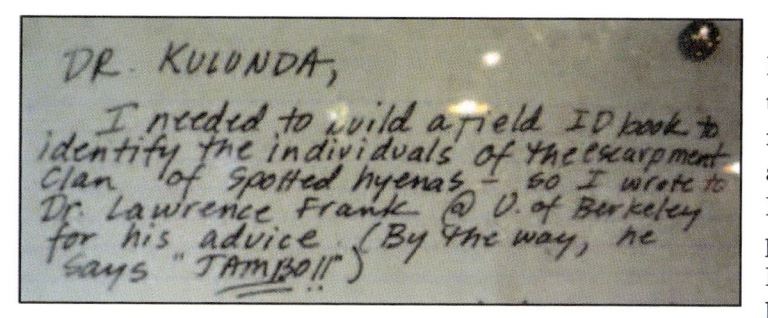

Professor Frank

In the Pangani Forest Exploration, a letter in the shack housing naked mole rats makes mention of Professor Lawrence [sic] Frank as a source of info for hyenas and their behavior. Laurence Frank (the correct spelling) is a professor at the University of California, Berkeley, who consulted with Disney about hyenas when constructing this park, and his name is mentioned here to lend authenticity to the fake letter correspondence on display.

Gorilla Falls

The original name of the Pangani Forest walking trail, Gorilla Falls, can still be seen on a crate near the gorilla observation area. This crate makes mention of the Gorilla Falls Conservation School. For those seeking a true intercultural connection, look for a reference to the same title in Swahili near the entrance to the walking trail.

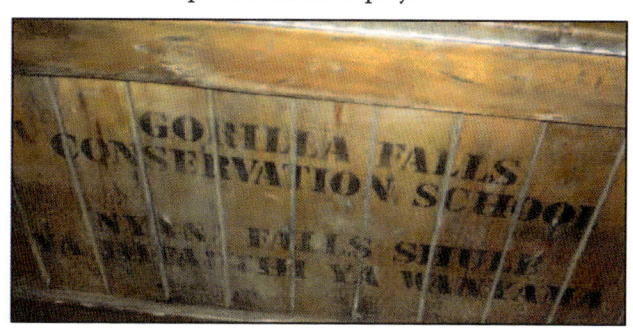

Affection Section Handwashing Stations

The bronze elephant statues seen on the Wildlife Express train platform at Rafiki's Planet Watch are formerly from the petting zoo area called Affection Section, where they served as the faucets which dispensed water for hand-washing on the way out. Proof can be seen by looking up the trunks of the metallic pachyderms—the metal grills are still there where water once gushed.

Disney's Animal Kingdom's Chief Designer

The Imagineer in charge of Disney's Animal Kingdom, Joe Rohde, is portrayed throughout Africa on weather-worn posters plastered to the outside of several buildings. Rohde is shown as a drawing of "Captain Bob", who advertises balloon rides over the safari. Those seeking closure and for the theming to come full-circle will revel in the discovery of an actual parachute, meant to be Captain Bob's, in the ceiling of the queue of Kilimanjaro Safari.

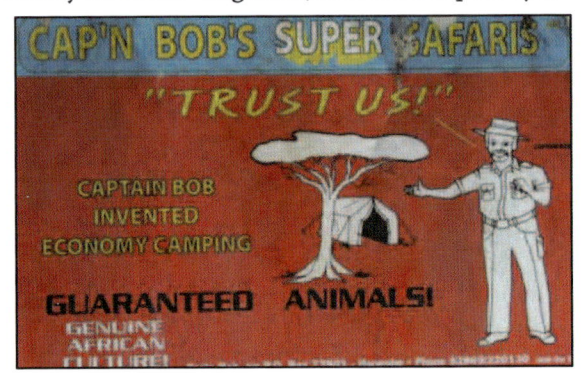

Jorodi Masks

Signs plastered on the walls of Harambe, along with other ads, pay further tribute to Joe Rohde. Artificially aged posters outside of Tusker House make mention of "Jorodi Masks and Beads," and the actual storefront for this supposed business—which sounds like "Joe Rohde" when spoken aloud—can be found in the main room of Tusker House in an upper story. As an added bonus, a sign at the storefront points out that they also specialize in earrings, a nod to the outrageous assortment of dangling earrings usually seen on Joe's left ear.

Disney Executive Frank Wells

One photograph in the FASTPASS queue for Expedition Everest shows former Disney executive Frank Wells near the base camp of Mt. Everest. An avid mountain climber, Wells had wanted to conquer the tallest mountain in all seven continents, which is why he is honored on the Magic Kingdom's Main Street windows with the phrase "Seven Summits Expedition." Wells succeeded on six of the seven continents; his two attempts to make it to the summit of Everest were unsuccessful. There is also a tribute to Wells in Disneyland's Matterhorn, where climbing gear is stamped "Wells Expedition" on one box.

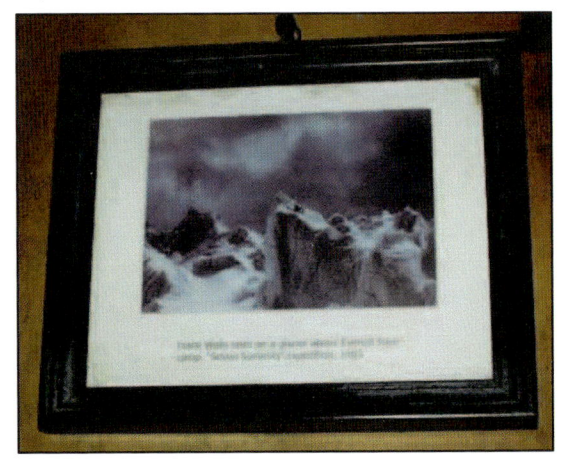

Imagineer Daniel Jue

The props in the queue for Expedition Everest were overseen by Imagineer Daniel Jue, who is immortalized in the photograph of the fictional Professor Pema Dorje (inspired by a real Dr. Pema Dorjee, a doctor in Tibet) seen near the doorway at the entrance to the yeti museum near the end of the queue. The supposed letter correspondence with Conservation International references not only a real organization, but also its real president, Russell Mittermeier.

Expedition Everest Team

The final sign in the standby queue of Expedition Everest mentions many names of people who worked on the project, including the chief designer of the park, Joe Rohde.

Chakranadi Chicken Shop

The addition in 2007 of Yak and Yeti heralded the first table-service restaurant in the park, which took the place of two quick-service locations, Sunaulo Toran Fries and Chakranadi Chicken Shop. One ornate wall of the distinctively-themed Chakranadi Chicken Shop was retained for the outdoor courtyard of the Yak and Yeti's counter-service operation, forging a link to the former inhabitant of this space. The Chakranadi Chicken Shop still appears on the town map across the walkway, near the ruined temple with monkeys on it.

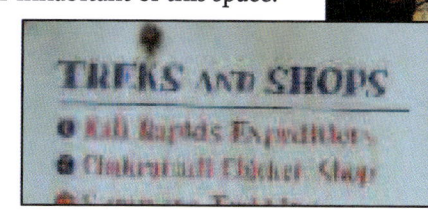

Kali Imagineers

A wooden paddle on a wall in the queue of Kali River Rapids was signed by all the Imagineers who built that attraction. The paddle can be seen in the final room of the covered structure in the queue, on the right side as you enter the room.

Tiger Rapids Run

One stone statue in the upramp of Kali River Rapids is a reminder of the ride's original theme and scope. When first conceived, the raft ride was going to be long, winding, and expansive, so that Asia would have a detailed ride with a lot of real estate along the same lines (if not the same actual scale) as Africa, which was home to Kilimanjaro Safari. The idea was to place the raft ride in immersive temple ruins holding the tiger enclosures, so that the tigers would only be visible from this attraction. When that concept was replaced by separated experiences (raft ride and tiger walk) while still in the planning stages, Kali River Rapids was scaled down, and only the stone tigers in the upramp remained as a silent homage to the original concept.

Disney's Animal Kingdom Opening Year

Highway signs in Chester and Hester's Dino-Rama honor the opening date of Disney's Animal Kingdom. Two signs label the main curving road of the land as Highway 498, which reference the opening date of Disney's Animal Kingdom on April 22, 1998. One sign sits near the Boneyard play area, while the other can be found near the road's dead-end alongside Primeval Whirl. A third reference to highway 498 can be seen off to the side of the large Dinosaur billboard at the very end of the road. A dedication plaque just outside the entrance to the Dino Institute makes a reference to April 22, 1978—a tribute to April 22, 1998, the day that Disney's Animal Kingdom opened. This portion of the institute is meant to portray an old-fashioned (and now out-dated) museum, and placing its supposed birth in the 1970s adds weight to the fiction.

Dinoland U.S.A. Backstory

The nearby fake gas pump, once located outside but now found inside the store, provides the key to Dinoland U.S.A.'s entire theme. The backstory to the land begins with Chester and Hester, who owned a sleepy gas station when dinosaur bones were discovered in the nearby archeological dig (the Boneyard play area). The success of that dig led scientists to take over a shack and expand it with their trailers; this is now known as Restaurantosaurus. The huge fossil dig also lured a modern museum, which houses the ride Dinosaur. Due in part to all their new neighbors and the traffic they attracted, Chester and Hester found it more profitable to sell dino trinkets to visitors than gas, so they converted their store. As sales soared, they expanded into the nearby "parking lot" and built midway games and carnival rides to entertain the travelers. Chester and Hester are displayed on a photo inside Restaurantosaurus.

Disney's Animal Kingdom Outline

The giant stegosaurus shoulder bone used to create the sign for the Boneyard is actually an outline of the original shape of Disney's Animal Kingdom. Before Asia was added, the park had a decidedly elongated shape, with a hump off to one side for Camp Minnie-Mickey. An "N" with an arrow on one side of the calcified marquee orients the viewer toward the north, and the bone's shape suddenly makes sense as the park's original outline. The Boneyard is site of an archeological dig by several professors and their students. Dr. Bernard Dunn, Dr. Shirley Woo, and Dr. Eugene McGee are joined by students Jenny Weinstein, Mark "Animal" Rios, and Sam Gonzales. Many of their stories can be read in bits and pieces in letters displayed in the dining rooms of Restaurantosaurus.

Former DVC Sales Outpost

Now used as a stopover point in parkwide quests and games for children, the hut between the Boneyard and Restaurantosaurus was once home to the Disney Vacation Club, where visitors could obtain general information about sales of the Disney timeshare company. One tidbit from the earlier resident remains; a crate just outside the hut is labeled "Ship to Disney's Old Key West Resort," in reference to one of the earliest DVC properties at Walt Disney World, Old Key West.

Imagineer Joe Rohde

The chief designer of Disney's Animal Kingdom has a subtle tribute at the Kid's Discovery station in Dinoland U.S.A., where the crate of bones is labeled "RD-1 Field Sample." That can be read aloud as "roadie" (if interchanging the "1" for an "I" as often happens in text messaging), which is the correct pronunciation of Rohde's last name. A less permanent homage to Rohde was previously scrawled in permanent marker on a blue barrel near Expedition Everest when Anandapur was first created.

Primeval World

Just inside the main dining room at Restaurantosaurus is a photo of Walt Disney with the dinosaurs from a 1964 World's Fair attraction. This is the same ride that eventually gave rise to the Primeval World addition of the Disneyland Railroad. Along the same wall, close to the restrooms, are line drawings from the Rite of Spring section of *Fantasia*, which famously staged a fight between an allosaurus and a stegosaurus and was eventually the inspiration for the climax of the Primeval World attraction as well. That same scene is reproduced in the main hall on a different wall, this time in the same pastel colors as the finished movie. It's also visible as a photograph on the wall in the gift shop at Dino-Rama.

Earth Day

The plaque at the entrance to Dinosaur honors Earth Day (April 22), in keeping with the conservation message of Disney's Animal Kingdom. Because the park has a mission of responsible stewardship of plants as well as animals, many ride and show elements lay emphasis on conservation, such as the anti-logging overtones of Kali River Rapids. But the park's only day-to-day reminder of the annual Earth Day celebration, which started in 1970, is this plaque outside of Dinosaur. The park intentionally opened on Earth Day in 1998.

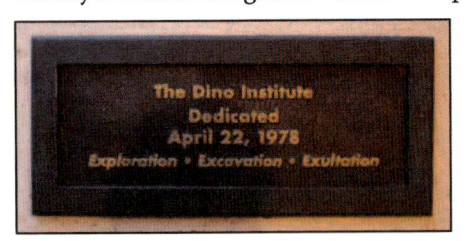

CTX

The attraction now known as Dinosaur was originally called Countdown to Extinction, and abbreviated CTX. The attraction was largely the same experience with a slightly different theme. Markings on the walls and vehicles in Dinosaur pay tribute to the attraction's first name. Parts of the walls and vehicles are still marked "CTX" in reference to the original name of the ride, and numerous references to extinction along the walls of the queue and shop at the exit also pay testament to the ride's original name. One sign on the wall as the ride starts reads WDI-AK98, which gives tribute to Walt Disney Imagineering and the park's opening year of 1998.

Countdown to Extinction Map

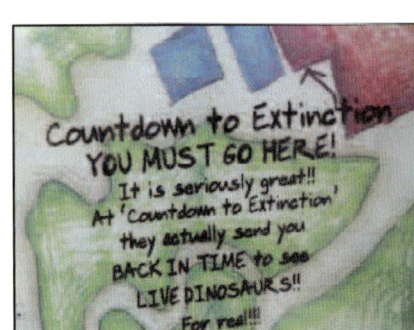

A map of the land located opposite Dino Dig still refers to the attraction building as Countdown to Extinction, not Dinosaur. It reads: "You must go here! It is seriously great!! At 'Countdown to Extinction' they actually send you BACK IN TIME to see LIVE DINOSAURS!! For real!!!" Over in Restaurantosaurus, a faux newspaper article next to the ordering stations not only shows the blueprint for the time rover, it mentions T-shirts emblazoned with "I survived extinction!", which made more sense when the ride was still called Countdown to Extinction.

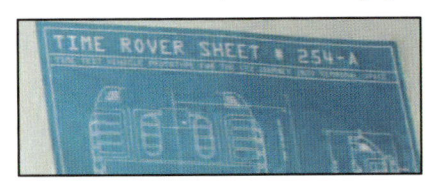

Dinoland U.S.A.'s Former Sponsor

Certain symbols in the ceiling at Dinosaur pay tribute to the original sponsor of the entire land. Pipes located overhead in several locations in the loading zone are labeled with the chemical formulas for ketchup, mustard, and mayonnaise, with even the pipes colored red, yellow, and white to further the gag. The reference to condiments honors McDonald's 1998-2008 sponsorship of the entire Dinoland U.S.A. region of the park. References to the food chain were common throughout the land. Food and drink containers with McDonald's logos were left, as if discarded, in places like the Boneyard's upstairs archeology office and the back seat of the "road trip" car near Dino-Rama. There were also McDonald's references alongside the model train in the ceiling of Chester and Hester's Dinosaur Treasures.

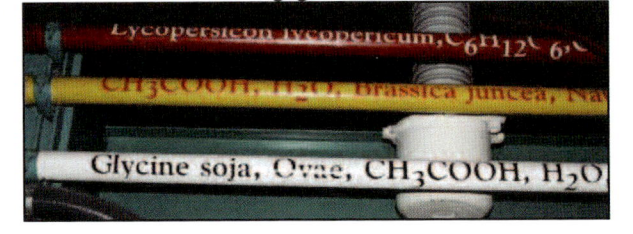

Toasters on Dinosaur

The time travel corridors in Dinosaur are scaled-up versions of heating coils from toasters. Disney designers always make a scale model of an attraction before building it; the innards of toasters were used in making the scale model of the two time-travel corridors, and the look of the actual ride was simply copied from the model. Strobe lights and sparks that accompany the effect were inspired by cigarette lighters, simply scaled up twenty times.

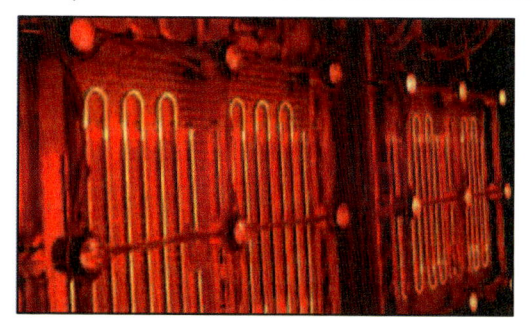

Dino-Pepper's Ghost

The mirror prominently displayed at the end of Dinosaur is a leftover from the original vision for the finale of the ride. Once upon a time, the idea was to have visitors see their own vehicle and the giant iguanodon ("one passenger, extra large") together in the mirror. Dr. Seeker's recorded voice saying "look who came back with you" was meant to reference the reflection in the mirror, to be accomplished via the same trick of light used for Haunted Mansion ballroom ghosts, an old magician's trick called Pepper's Ghost. Since the effect could not be convincingly portrayed, a security camera was instead installed to show the dinosaur in our time period, and the mirror sits unused.

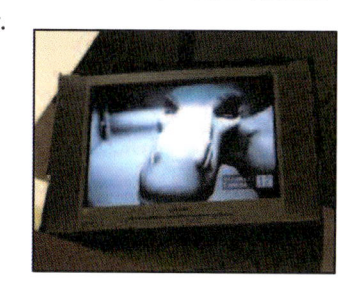

Dinosaur Jubilee

The giant turtle-shaped replica dinosaur skeleton hanging from the ceiling in the gift shop at the exit to Dinosaur is an artifact from a previous attraction. The space now occupied by Chester and Hester's Dino-Rama was originally home to Dinosaur Jubilee, a walk-through exhibit of dinosaur skeletons inside a large tent, ostensibly harvested from the dinosaur dig in the kids' playground. Many replica skeletons of popular dinosaurs were included, and the turtle-type skeleton was later transported to the gift shop.

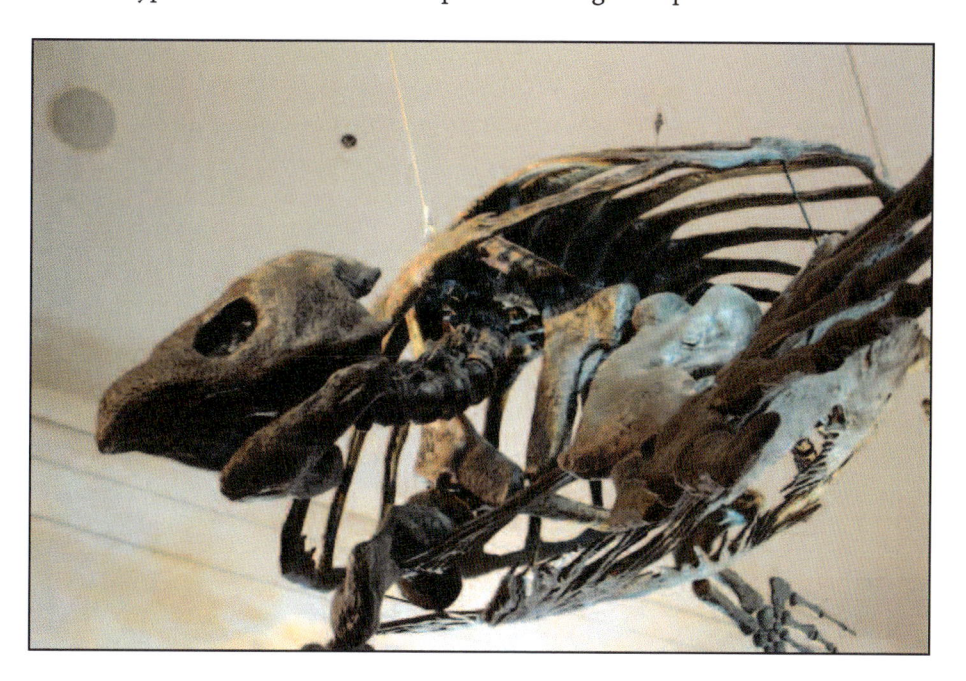

General Walt Disney World

Mogul Mania

The snow blowers in the Ski Patrol Training Camp section of Blizzard Beach are functional remnants of a former attraction in this area. As first conceived, the area now used for standard inner tube waterslides was a more freestyle experience called Mogul Mania, in which inner tubes simply navigated down moguls (snow bumps) with no predetermined path, leading to much variation and also airtime—so much airtime that injuries were reported early and the area had to be shut down and re-thought. Since the moguls had been hard material rather than snow, they had to be kept wet, so the snow blowers sprayed water on the entire area. The snow blowers today serve only a thematic function, but are the same ones in use when Mogul Mania was here.

Lagoon Wave Machine

Early Walt Disney World executives wanted "the Vacation Kingdom" to feature amenities unique in the world, so they built a wave machine at one island in the Seven Seas Lagoon in order to generate excitement along the beaches of the Polynesian Resort. It never really worked as desired, however, because the waves rapidly eroded the beaches at the Polynesian. The machinery went silent not too long after its first use, but it remains at the bottom of the lagoon, not too far offshore from the Polynesian Resort.

Father of the Bride

A facility at the wedding pavilion near Grand Floridian was named after a movie character. Franck's Bridal Studio (built in 1995) is named after the Martin Short character in *Father of the Bride*—he played a wedding planner, of course.

Discovery Island

The island in the middle of Bay Lake (which is not a man-made lake) was once used as a separate attraction at Walt Disney World, celebrating close encounters with exotic animals, especially birds. It had previously had light pirate theming and was known as Blackbeard's Island and Treasure Island, until 1977 when it became a wildlife mini-park. Discovery Island closed a year after Disney's Animal Kingdom opened in 1998.

River Country

An overgrown series of slides adjacent to Fort Wilderness was once a water park called River Country. The idea to capture an old-fashioned "watering hole" drew a healthy stream of visitors for many years, but after Blizzard Beach joined Typhoon Lagoon as even-larger water parks on Disney's roster, River Country closed forever.

Carolwood Pacific Railroad

A couple of the passenger cars from Walt Disney's personal home miniature railroad, the Carolwood-Pacific, are on display in the DVC wing of the Wilderness Lodge. These are actual cars used at Walt's Holmby Hills home; rider would sit directly on top of these cars.

Imagineer Mary Blair

Known for creating the dolls of "it's a small world," Mary Blair also designed the murals that adorn the central column of the Contemporary Resort, and her signature is scrawled on one tile near the entrance to the restaurants on the fourth floor. There are 18,000 tiles on this mural on the Grand Canyon Concourse. Nearby tiles also commemorate her team and others who worked on the murals at the Contemporary. The full list of names reads: Mary Blair, deLarioe, D. Tousley, K. Leix Troost, Brooke B., Juanita J., L. Palmer, V. Ringer, M. Spence, T. O'Brien, D. Mahoney, D. Garden, L. Marshall, and Fawzi Zein. Photos of Blair herself, plus a few more prints of her artwork, were added to the California Grill's Monterrey Room in 2013.

Fort Wilderness Railroad

The water tower structure at the pool in Fort Wilderness's Meadow section includes a WRR design—a holdover from the narrow-gauge Fort Wilderness Railroad that operated at this resort until the early 1980s. Almost all the track has been removed, but some of the right-of-way cleared path can still be seen. The locomotive once used here was involved in a complex series of trades to finally grant Disneyland a fifth engine, the Ward Kimball.

The Gully Whumper Keel Boat

The Mike Fink Keel Boats, which until 1997 whipped around the Rivers of America, are honored in the Trail's End restaurant at Fort Wilderness. There are small-scale models of keel boats in display boxes that provide an indirect link, but a more direct homage can be found in a piece of the Gully Whumper boat itself from the Magic Kingdom.

Earl of Sandwich Opening Day Photo

In one corner of the dining room (near the connector to the shop on one side) is a photograph of the actual Earl of Sandwich from the United Kingdom, present at the Downtown Disney eatery on its first day of operation.

The First Characters in Flight

Some of the silhouetted figures in the ticket booth building for the balloon rides at Downtown Disney are not represented on the balloon at all, but are leftovers from the design of the first balloon. When the up-charge attraction premiered in 2009, it featured a balloon with silhouette designs on it, using clearly recognizable Disney characters who take flight, such as Peter Pan, Dumbo, Buzz Lightyear, and Mary Poppins. While some of the same characters returned when a new balloon debuted in 2012, Peter Pan and Dumbo did not, and their presence on the ticket booth is the only reminder of the early balloon design.

Mighty Ducks of Anaheim

A bronze figure atop a column at the entrance to DisneyQuest is a remnant of the time when the Disney company owned the Mighty Ducks of Anaheim hockey team. Originally created by Disney (and its then-CEO Michael Eisner), the Mighty Ducks later became a standalone franchise, but the human-hockey game in DisneyQuest already used the Ducks mascot, and a bronze version of this mascot still exists at the entrance to the arcade.

Treasure of the Incas

Two physical reminders in the first floor of DisneyQuest can be traced back to the original occupant of this space. The hollow sound of the floorboards in the safari video game section is due to the Plexiglas below, for this space was once home to a remote-controlled car attraction that took place in the floor, right below visitors' feet. Called Treasure of the Incas, this attraction let people drive the remote controlled jeeps through a maze of tiny rooms, using consoles off to the side of the room, in search of the rare room with tiny treasure piled in it. Navigation was difficult to do by looking through the Plexiglas floor, but each jeep helpfully had a video camera installed, so a live feed could be seen at the driving station. A more visible artifact of this attraction can be seen in the center of the room today, in the form of a "stone" column with the inscription "Search for Treasure Rooms" and a representation of a doorway similar to one a jeep might enter.

Alien Encounter

One room-sized video game, almost a ride, at DisneyQuest takes place in the same fictional universe as the former Magic Kingdom ride, the ExtraTERRORestrial Alien Encounter. This video game, called Invasion, places riders inside an oversized, spider-like planetary crawler called X-S 5000. The experience explicitly mentions its origins from the company X-S Tech, the same company supposedly responsible for the ExtraTERRORestrial Alien Encounter.

Cake Castle

One game in DisneyQuest, Living Easels, lets children "paint" onto pre-made backgrounds and characters, and one such background pays subtle tribute to Walt Disney World history. The background shows Cinderella Castle covered in icing and candles as if it were a giant birthday cake. Indeed, this very event took place in 1996, when the castle was decorated in honor of the Magic Kingdom's 25th Anniversary.

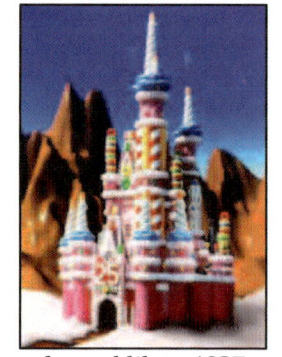

Pleasure Island Statues

The monkey prop in D-Street at Downtown Disney comes from the onetime club on Pleasure Island called Adventurers Club. That facility had been themed like a 1937-era bar for world explorers and thus was crammed with artifacts from around the globe. The club closed in 2008, and some of the props made their way eventually to D-Street to add to the decorations already on display. In addition to the monkey, look also for Scooter the Peacock and a headless suit of armor as two other prominent props that came from Pleasure Island.

Colonel's Cotton Mill

The cotton flower visible on the large mural at the Riverside Mill is a remnant of the time when this restaurant was known as Colonel's Cotton Mill, and the entire resort was called Dixie Landings. When Port Orleans expanded in 2002 to encompass Dixie Landings (then renamed to Port Orleans Riverside), the Colonel's Cotton Mill became the Riverside Mill.

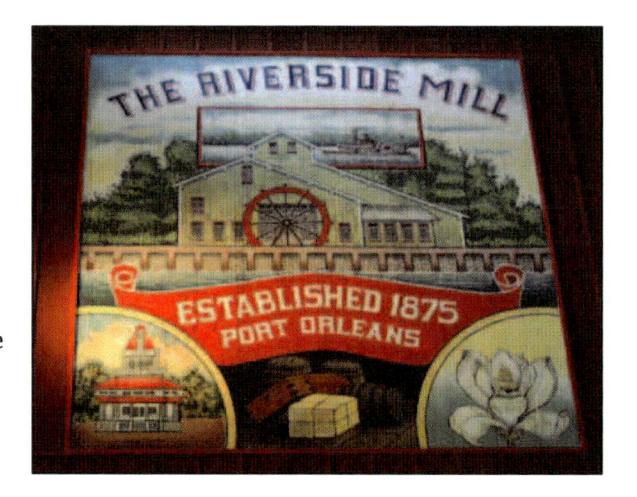

Luna Park Creator

Dundy's Sundries at the BoardWalk Inn is named after Skip Dundy, the creator of Luna Park. One of the theme parks of Coney Island in its heyday, Luna Park was famous for its nighttime vistas of thousands of white lights on its midway and for its renowned coaster, the Cyclone. Much of BoardWalk's design aesthetic mirrors Luna Park.

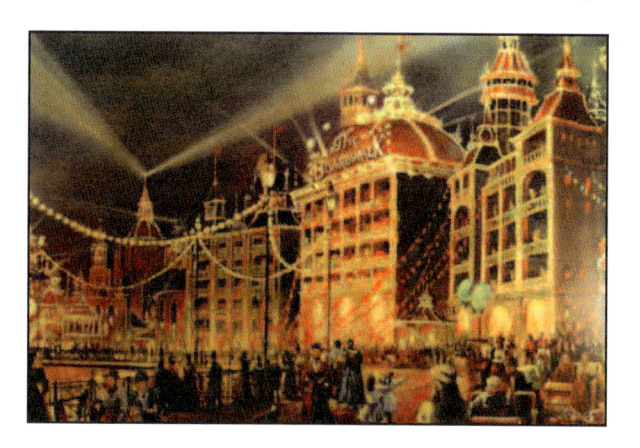

Hidden Mickey Guy

A tribute in the food court of All Stars Sports honors the author of the "Hidden Mickey" books, Steve Barrett, by including his likeness amid the redone decorations and windows from a 2013 refurbishment. Barrett is not an employee of Disney but just a fan who wrote independent guides on finding Hidden Mickeys around the parks, and impressed the Imagineers enough to warrant his own homage. His cartoon image can be found on the far side of the Mickey-playing-hockey window in the food court dining area, wearing his trademark hat and holding a thin yellow book like the ones he writes.

Attraction Dates

<u>Current Attractions</u>
Astro Orbiter (1994-present)
Barnstormer at Goofy's Wiseacre Farm (1996-present)
Big Thunder Mountain Railroad (1975-present)
Buzz Lightyear's Space Ranger Spin (1998-present)
Casey Jr. Splash 'N' Soak Station (2012-present)
Country Bear Jamboree (1971-present)
Dumbo the Flying Elephant (1971-present)
Enchanted Tales with Belle (2012-present)
Frontierland Shootin' Arcade (1971-present)
Hall of Presidents (1971-present)
Haunted Mansion (1971-present)
it's a small world (1971-present)
Jungle Cruise (1971-present)
Liberty Square Riverboat / Liberty Belle (1996-present)
Mad Tea Party (1971-present)
Magic Carpets of Aladdin (2001-present)
Main Street Vehicles (1971-present)
Many Adventures of Winnie the Pooh (1999-present)
Mickey's Philharmagic (2003-present)
Monsters, Inc. Laugh Floor (2007-present)
Peter Pan's Flight (1971-present)
Pirates of the Caribbean (1973-present)
Prince Charming Regal Carrousel (2010-present)
Seven Dwarfs Mine Train (2014-present)
Sorcerers of the Magic Kingdom (2012-present)
Space Mountain (1975-present)
Splash Mountain (1992-present)
Stitch's Great Escape (2004-present)
Swiss Family Treehouse (1971-present)
Tom Sawyer Island (1973-present)
Tomorrowland Speedway (1971-present)
Tomorrowland Transit Authority PeopleMover (1975-present)
Treasures of the Seven Seas (2013-present)
Walt Disney World Railroad (1971-present)
Walt Disney's Carousel of Progress (1975-present)
Walt Disney's Enchanted Tiki Room (2011-present)

Agent P's World Showcase Adventure (2012-present)
American Adventure (1982-present)
Captain EO (1986-1994; 2010-present)
Circle of Life: An Environmental Fable (1995-present)
Ellen's Energy Adventure (1996-present)
Gran Fiesta Tour (2007-present)
ImageWorks - The "What If" Labs (1982-present)
Impressions de France (1982-present)
Innoventions (1994-present)
Journey Into Imagination With Figment (2002-present)
Living with the Land (1993-present)
Maelstrom (1988-present)
Mission: SPACE (2003-present)
O Canada! (1982-present)
Reflections of China (2003-present)
Soarin' (2005-present)
Spaceship Earth (1982-present)
Test Track (1999-present)
The Seas with Nemo & Friends (2006-present)
Turtle Talk with Crush (2004-present)

Backlot Tour (1989-present)
Beauty and the Beast – Live on Stage (1991-present)
Disney Junior – Live on Stage (2011-present)
Fantasmic! (1998-present)
Great Movie Ride (1989-present)
Honey I Shrunk the Kids Movie Set Adventure (1990-present)
Indiana Jones Epic Stunt Spectacular (1989-present)
Jedi Training Academy (2007-present)
Legend of Captain Jack Sparrow (2012-present)
Lights, Motors, Action! Extreme Stunt Show (2005-present)
Magic of Disney Animation (2003-present)
MuppetVision 3-D (1991-present)
One Man's Dream (2001-present)
Rock 'n' Roller Coaster (1999-present)
Star Tours (1989-present)
Toy Story Midway Mania (2008-present)
Twilight Zone Tower of Terror (1994-present)
Voyage of the Little Mermaid (1992-present)

Dinosaur (2000-present)
Expedition Everest - Legend of the Forbidden Mountain (2006-present)
Festival of the Lion King (1998-present)
Finding Nemo – The Musical (2006-present)
Flights of Wonder (1998-present)
It's Tough to be a Bug (1998-present)

Kali River Rapids (1999-present)
Kilimanjaro Safari (1998-present)
Primeval Whirl (2002-present)
Rafiki's Planet Watch (1999-present)
TriceraTop Spin (2001-present)

Former Attractions
20,000 Leagues Under the Sea (1971-1994)
ABC Sound Studio (1997-1999)
America the Beautiful (1975-1984)
American Idol Experience (2008-2014)
American Journeys (1984-1994)
Backstage Pass (1990-2001)
Cinderella's Golden Carrousel (1971-2010)
CommuniCore (1982-1994)
Conservation Station (1998-1999)
Countdown to Extinction (1998-2000)
Country Bear Christmas Special (1984-2006)
Country Bear Vacation Hoedown (1986-2001)
Davy Crockett Explorer Canoes (1971-1994)
Diamond Horseshoe Jamboree (1986-1995)
Diamond Horseshoe Revue (1971-1986)
Diamond Horseshoe Saloon Revue (1995-2003)
Dick Tracy Diamond Double-Cross (1990-1991)
Dinosaur Jubilee (1998-2000)
Discovery Island (1977-1998)
Disney's DOUG Live! (1999-2001)
Donald's Boat (1996-2011)
Dreamflight (1989-1996)
El Rio Del Tiempo (1982-2007)
Enchanted Tiki Room Under New Management (1998-2011)
ExtraTERRORestrial Alien Encounter (1995-2003)
Flight to the Moon (1971-1975)
Food Rocks (1994-2004)
Get Happy with ABC (2002-2002)
Goosebumps HorrorLand Fright Show and FunHouse (1997-1998)
Here Come the Muppets (1990-1991)
Honey, I Shrunk the Audience (1994-2010)
Horizons (1983-1999)
Hunchback of Notre Dame: A Musical Adventure (1996-2002)
If You Could Fly (1987-1989)
If You Had Wings (1972-1987)
Journey into Imagination (1983-1998)
Journey into Jungle Book (1998-1999)
Journey into Narnia (2008-2011)
Journey into Your Imagination (1998-2002)

Kim Possible World Showcase Adventure (2006-2012)
Kitchen Kabaret (1982-1994)
Legend of the Lion King (1994-2002)
Listen to the Land (1982-1993)
Living Seas (1986-2004)
Magic Carpet 'Round the World (1974-1975)
Magic Journeys (1982-1986; 1987-1994)
Main Street Cinema (1971-1998)
Mickey Mouse Revue (1971-1980)
Mickey's Birthdayland (1988-1990)
Mickey's Country House (1988-2011)
Mickey's Hollywood Theater (1988-1996)
Mickey's Starland (1990-1996)
Mike Fink Keel Boats (1971-1997)
Minnie's Country House (1988-2011)
Mission to Mars (1975-1993)
Monster Sound Show (1989-1997)
Mr. Toad's Wild Ride (1971-1998)
Playhouse Disney Live (2001-2011)
Plaza Swan Boats (1973-1983)
River Country (1976-2002)
Show Biz Is (1989-1990)
Skyway (1971-1999)
Snow White's Scary Adventures (1971-2012)
Sounds Dangerous (1999-2012)
Spirit of Pocahontas (1995-1996)
Star Jets (1974-1994)
Superstar Television (1989-1999)
Symbiosis (1982-1995)
Take Flight (1989-1996)
Tarzan Rocks (1999-2006)
Timekeeper (1994-2006)
Tomorrowland Transit Authority (1994-2010)
Tomorrowland Grand Prix Raceway (1971-1996)
Treasure Island (1974-1977)
Tropical Serenade (1971-1997)
Universe of Energy (1982-1996)
Walt Disney Story (1973-1992)
WEDway PeopleMover (1975-1994)
Who Wants to be a Millionaire-Play it! (2001-2006)
Wonders of China (1982-2003)
Wonders of Life (1989-2004)
World of Motion (1982-1996)

Main Street Windows

There are enough individuals honored on Main Street to warrant a complete listing. Here they are, listed one side of the street at a time.

West Main Street (from the fire station up toward the castle)

Roger Broggie
Owen Pope
Buddy Baker
Bob Jackman
George Bruns
Ron Logan
Lonnie Lindley
Ed Bullard
Robert Jani
Charles Corson
Emile Kuri
Charlie Ridgway
Joyce Carlson
Bob Booth
Roger Broggie Jr.
John Frankie
Neil Gallagher
Jack Gladish
Rudy Pena
Dave Schweninger
Dick Van Every
Jim Verity
Morrie Houser
Lou Jennings
John Joyce
Don Edgren
John Wise
Ken Klug
Stan Maslak
John Zovich
David Snyder
Michael Bagnall
Bill Walsh

Cecil Robinson
Jack Lindquist
Dave Gengenbach
Bob Gurr
George McGinnis
Bill Watkins
Earl Vilmer
Card Walker
Ted Crowell
Arnold Lindberg
Claude Coats
Marc Davis
John DeCuir
Bill Justice
Jim Armstrong
John Curry
Howard Roland
Stan Garves
Tony Baxter
Dave Burkhart
Ed Johnson
Gary Younger
Ralph Kent

East Main Street (from the Plaza Restaurant toward Town Square)

Larry Slocum
Walt Disney
Howard Brummitt
Marvin Davis
Vic Green
John Hench
Fred Hope
Richard Irvine
Bill Martin
Chuck Myall
Bill Sullivan
Bob Matheison
Christopher Miller
Jennifer Miller
Joanna Miller
Patrick Miller
Ron and Diane Miller
Ronald Miller Jr.
Tamara Miller
Walter Miller
Don Iwerks
Ub Iwerks
Bill Washo
Bud Washo
Dick Nunis
Ron Miller
Orlando Ferrante
Abigail Disney
Roy Patrick Disney
Patty Disney
Roy E. Disney
Susan Disney
Timothy Disney
Morgan Evans
Tony Virginia
Donn Tatum
Frank Wells
Carl Bongirno
Jim McManus
Warren Robertson
Larry Tryon
Neal McClure
Dick Morrow

Spence Olin
Jim Ross
Phil Smith
Bonar Dyer
Hank Dains
Chuck Fowler
Frank Millington
Marshall Smelser
Bill Sullivan
Bob Matheison
Bob Allen
Pete Crimmings
Dick Evans
Bill Joelscher
Jack Olsen
Pete Clark
Jack Sayers
Norm Fagrell
Bud Dare
Mary Blair
Collin Campbell
Blaine Gibson
Dorothea Redmond
Herb Ryman
Nolan Browning
Roy Davis (aka Roy O. Disney)
Bob Price (aka Bob Foster)
Elias Disney
Ken Chapman
Paul Hartley
Sam McKim
Elmer Plummer
Ernie Prinzhorn
Vince Jefferds
Lou Tonarely
Wilbur Watt
Bradford Lund
Michelle Lund
Victoria Lund
William and Sharon Lund

Malcolm Cobb
Jack Ferges
Fred Joerger
Mitz Natsume
Bob Sewell
Lee Cockerell
Bruce Laval
Tom Eastman
James Passilla
Pat Vaughn
Tom Nabbe
Yale Gracey
Bud Martin
Ken O'Brien
Wathel Rogers
Bill Bosche
Jack Boyd
Bob Bigeaut
Dick Pfahler
McLaren Steward
Robert Moore
Norm Noceti
Ed Chisholm
Gordon Williams
X Atencio
Al Bertino
Marty Sklar
Doug Cayne
Joe Kramer
George Windrum
Ron Bowman
Glenn Durflinger
Don Holmquist
Dick Kline
George Nelson
Roy O. Disney
Joe Potter
Bill Irwin
Larry Reiser
Pete Markham
Dan Dingman
Francis Stanek
Bob Phelps

Ken Creekmore
Orpha Harryman
John Keehne
Alyja Paskevicius
Tom Peirce

Bonus Chapter: History at Universal Studios Florida

Islands of Adventure

- Every "island" (themed zone) of Islands of Adventure is based upon a book of some kind, such as comic books, children's books, or novels.

- The Hulk is meant to provide patrons with the "roller coaster of emotions" that results when the gamma sled experiments to restore Dr. Banner go awry.

- The tubular rails of roller coasters are usually filled with materials to dampen the noise. At the Hulk, the loud roar is intentional to match the theme, and the rails were left hollow. At Dragon Challenge, the tubes are filled with peat gravel to provide the aural sensation of animalistic flight.

- When first built, the linear induction motors (LIM) that provide the launch to the Hulk generated such a strong magnetic field that any credit cards brought on board by riders were demagnetized. Since that would have ruined the day at the park, this had to be redesigned before opening.

- The delay riders experience on the lift of the Hulk is actually time used to weigh the car, so a computer can decide the amount of thrust needed. A heavier car will be accelerated faster; up to 60 MPH in just 1.8 seconds.

- Another Marvel superhero lurks in Spider-Man: Iron Man shows up two times in the Spider-Man ride—he can be seen in the first room with a 3-D screen, painted near the top of a building, and he is visible again near the end of the ride, as our vehicle is being dragged around. Watch the bottom-right of the screen for an advertisement from Stark Industries that includes Iron Man.

- A phone number visible in the Spider-Man ride is an actual phone line maintained by Universal Studios, just to reward sharp-eyed visitors with cell phones. Right before our ascent into the skyscrapers during the final scenes of the ride, Spider-Man clings to a theater's marquee, on which a phone number is visible. If visitors later call the displayed numbers, 407-224-1783, they will hear this recorded message: "Thank you for calling the Coup Theater. Due to the recent unpleasantness caused by Doc Ock and his gang of villains, we will be closed until further notice… or at least until Spider-Man can make our city safe again. Beep!" This phone number once belonged to Thierry Coup, the creative director for the Spider-Man attraction. The name of the theater is a further tribute to Coup.

- An oversized sandstone wall along the major pathway in Jurassic Park, near the Discovery Center, blocks a smaller walkway that once led to an attraction called Triceratops Encounter. Park visitors would be ushered into a small room where a full-sized triceratops rested sedately within reach. This robotic performer wiggled, blinked, snorted, and moved in many small ways to convey the sense of reality. To commemorate the extinct attraction, which closed in 2004, designers inscribed the sandstone blocking the walkway with triceratops bones.

- A boat dock in Jurassic Park's waterside jungles is a remnant of a former attraction called Island Skipper Tours, which used to transport visitors across the lagoon to the park's entrance. To save patrons the trouble of walking the half-circle needed to exit the park (or that same distance at the start of the day), boats were used to make the journey more quickly. They closed in 2002.

- A representation of Dr. Seuss himself can be seen in Seuss Landing. Just opposite the entrance to the High in the Sky Trolley is a photo location with a statue of a policeman; just above that are three mayoral figures carved on the wall. The one on the left, wearing glasses, sports the visage of Theodor Geisel (1904-1991), the real-life author whose pseudonym was Dr. Seuss.

- The buildings in Seuss Landing are made from Styrofoam. For proof of the strange heritage in its building materials, simply knock on any wall with your knuckles, and it should sound hollow. The rounded look of the buildings was accomplished by using chain saws to individually sculpt every façade.

- The High in the Sky Seuss Trolley Train Ride may have opened in 2006, but the track had sat empty since 1999 because the original concept, individual cars called "Sylvester McMonkey McBean's Very Unusual Driving Machines," could not be built due to safety concerns.

Universal Studios Florida

- Mouse Ears on the tires of a car at Twister provide a tongue-in-cheek reference to Orlando's other big theme park operator. In the queue of Twister, a car dangles from the ceiling, with one wheel still spinning as if disaster has just occurred. On that tire is a familiar hat with Mouse Ears, as if implying the car had run over someone who had visited the competition!

- The sounds of the tornado in Twister were not merely recorded from a live storm. Rather, designers took the sounds of animals and contorted them. Incongruously, to get the sound we now hear, they mixed the howls of a lion, a camel, and a monkey, stretched the mixture, and played it backwards.

- The exit doors of Twister are vacuum sealed. This is not by design; it's an unintentional by-product of all the pressure that builds up inside the attraction each time it operates.

- The funnel cloud in Twister is a real vortex, not an optical illusion or special effect. The barometric pressure of the outside weather plays a role as well. On days with poor weather and low pressure, the vortex inside the attraction will be thicker.

- The New York streets are a direct result of director Steven Spielberg's experiences as a young man in Universal Studios-Hollywood. When he was an aspiring filmmaker, Spielberg took the standard tourist tram tour in the Hollywood park, but he was disillusioned that the tram didn't actually see any filming going on. So he snuck off the tram tour and set out on his own, eventually camping out in an unused bungalow and essentially squatting on the Universal property. Though several insiders knew what he was up to, they allowed him to stay, and soon enough Spielberg had real movies (and instant hits) to his name, and his presence became legitimate. When he was tapped to help design the Orlando park, Spielberg remembered the problem of a tram tour where the filming action took place in the "back lot," so he increased the likelihood of tourists seeing filming by building those sets in the "front lot," right at the theme park, in the first place.

- The New York streets reproduce several famous façades from movies. The Empire Hotel is from *Vertigo*, the café is from *Batteries Not Included*, and there are façades from *Annie*, *The Sting*, and *West Side Story* as well.

- The former occupant of the building which now houses the Mummy is commemorated inside the Mummy's treasure room. Since Kongfrontation was the ride originally taking up this space, designers included a two-foot tall golden statue of King Kong in this room. Look for it on the left side, just past the halfway point in the room, high up near the ceiling.

- The hieroglyphics on the walls of the queue use authentic symbols and warn of Imhotep. The hieroglyphics in the treasure room are also authentic, but these pay further homage to King Kong, with phrases such as "Kong is watching you" and "Kong will never die." There are also hieroglyphics that provide directions to the Mummy coaster's control booth.

- When King Kong was present in the park, an artificial odor was pumped into the room where park visitors came face to face with him. Universal even trademarked this scent, which went by the name of

Banana Breath. Other Universal-trademarked odors include Burnt Shark (used at the Jaws ride) and Musty Forest (used at the E.T. attraction).

- The "fake ending" of the Mummy, where the ride attendant is seemingly killed in front of us, was a gag originally written for a Stephen King ride that never came to fruition. The idea was kept around at Universal Creative, the arm of the company that designs theme parks, in keeping with a philosophy of not throwing any good idea away and recycling them when possible into other projects.

- The predecessor to Disaster! was simply called Earthquake, and the new Disaster! attraction keeps the focus in the finale on the temblor. Although the new attraction focuses on different kinds of disasters, the final scene was left intact from the original ride, so visitors only experience an earthquake and its related effects, such as fire and flood.

- The London façades and Diagon Alley were once home to Jaws, and small references to Amity Island can still be seen on neighboring buildings near Disaster! The record store façade of London includes an album by the Quint Trio called "Here's to Swimmin' with Bow-Legged Women," a reference to a line from the first *Jaws* movie. Inside Diagon Alley, a store named Mr. Mulpepper's Apothecary has shark jaws in the window as an intentional tribute. Finally, a telescope above the doorway in Wiseacre's Wizarding Equipment was built partially using pieces of an old boat from the Jaws attraction, including the seat.

- Men in Black is designed to look like a World's Fair exhibit but function in reality as a training facility for the alien-fighting program. Only three endings were written for Will Smith to record, but in the studio he improvised over fifty different endings for the ride. It takes exotic situations, like really diverse results between the two cars, to hear the unusual recordings. The pithy comments when a team scores especially low include "you zigged when you should have zagged" and "the Men in PINK is right down the street."

- Look for Steven Spielberg himself, the maestro behind the Florida version of the Universal Studios park, to be represented as a cardboard cutout on a bus in the first training portion of Men in Black.

- The Simpsons Ride honors the former occupant of this space, the Back to the Future Ride, in multiple ways in the queue. Christopher Lloyd, the actor who portrayed Doc Emmett Brown in the *Back to the Future* movies, lent his voice to a cartoon version of himself that plays briefly on the overhead monitors. In this skit, Professor Frink (the scientist on the Simpsons) goes to visit the Institute of Future Technology and sees instead the same Krustyland façade we passed through a minute ago. Depressed, he realizes he can't see Doc Brown, his hero… unless he travels back in time with a Delorean. He hops in one conveniently nearby, and zooms back two years ago. As he materializes, he runs over a man next to Doc Brown. Turns out Doc Brown was about to sign a contract for a small business loan, which would enable him to keep the Institute of Future Technology open. So Professor Frink has actually caused Doc Brown to go out of business! Krusty shows up, and promptly hires Doc Brown as a ticket-taker for his new park, since Krusty is going to own the land.

- The really sharp visitors can also hear a quick reminder of the Back to the Future experience. Originally, Doc told us just before we boarded the cars that the psychopath Biff Tannen was running loose in the facility. In the Simpsons Ride, Krusty says much the same thing about Sideshow Bob and a psychopath loose in the area.

- The Simpsons Ride itself also pays homage to Back to the Future. In the original Back to the Future Ride, a dinosaur ate our vehicle in a distinctive one-two swallowing motion before our escape, and this is repeated by giant Maggie attempting to use our car as a pacifier. Not coincidentally, this is occurring at an outdoor square in Springfield that ought to look familiar; it's a cartoon version of the famous square and courthouse from *Back to the Future* (you can see the clock tower clearly).

- E.T. the Extra-Terrestrial Adventure is the last original ride in Universal Studios Florida, which opened in 1989.

- The cityscape model we fly over in E.T. was built in Atlanta and designed to break apart into three parts so it could fit through the large hangar doors of the attraction. However, when it arrived, it still wouldn't fit, so the entire model had to be painstakingly disassembled and reassembled after all—a process that took an additional three months.

- Except for the building housing Terminator 2: 3-D Battle Across Time, all the façades in the area were inspired by real buildings in Hollywood. The villas at the end of the street are reproductions of the hotel that was the first ever to feature private bathrooms, and had been owned by a silent film actress. Until the Terminator attraction was opened in 1996, the street was home to a sedate tram tour that navigated the park right in the same area as tourists walked.

- The theater housing Shrek 4-D was once home to Alfred Hitchcock Presents, a celebration of moviemaking by the famous Hollywood director. With Shrek, the theater took on a decidedly more snarky tone. Faux movie posters in the queue, for instance, poke fun at Disney park attractions such as Dumbo the flying elephant.

Afterword

Every year, about thirty million people visit Walt Disney World, making it one of the top tourist destinations in the United States. Disney built its theme parks in the middle of nowhere, and still the people descended in droves. The number of visitors is possibly a better choice than any other tidbit to encapsulate the message of this book: people will come in record numbers to experience the magic Disney produces, and central to the Disney magic are these details and tributes, a combined reverence for the past and for historical accuracy. Those details create the "Disney Difference" which draws people and keeps them coming back for more every year.

While many patrons consciously think only about the rides at Walt Disney World, it's the rich sub-culture of homages, tributes, fun details, intricate trivia, and rich backstories at the parks which do the heavy lifting of enchanting our imaginations.

The Disney attention to detail is legendary, and rightly so. Only by exposing the level to which these details are researched, sought after, refined, and finally implemented can we begin to understand the richness of the tapestry at a Disney theme park. The persuasive tricking of our senses, the completely believable immersion into fictitious realms, and the unconditional suspension of disbelief all owe their existence to such details that seem, at first glance, to be mere adornments, or perhaps even indulgences by the artists.

Don't be fooled. It's the details at Disney that render the experience magical. To know the details is to examine the magician's trick hat—you will have a fuller understanding of what's going on and what to watch for, and it will only increase your enjoyment of the effect.

Kevin Yee

About the Author

Kevin Yee spent more than a decade working at Disneyland and cultivating a never-ending fascination with that park's rich traditions and history. Now relocated to Central Florida, Kevin has visited the Walt Disney World parks more than 1,000 times. He also enjoys traveling to the Disney parks in other countries.

Kevin is the author (or co-author) of several Disney books:

- *Mouse Trap: Memoir of a Disneyland Cast Member*. This affectionate recounting of fifteen years of working for Disneyland on the front lines provides an inside glimpse at life working for the Mouse, including its perks and its rewards, and allows those on the outside to imagine what life is like on the inside of the "trap."
- *Epcot—The First Thirty Years*. An unofficial fan retrospective of Epcot and EPCOT Center from 1982-2012. Featuring over 500 photos (the book is available in color or black/white versions), this provides a fan's perspective of the changes over the years and the attractions and entertainment we remember now with our stories and images.
- *Walt Disney World 'Earbook*. An annual publication detailing the changes at Walt Disney World over the past calendar year, starting in 2010 and continuing to the present.
- *Top Tips for Visiting the Tokyo Disney Resort*. This guide to Tokyo Disneyland and Tokyo DisneySea takes all the guesswork out of a journey to Japan and the phenomenal Disney parks there. You'll have step by step guidelines for what to do and what to expect, so there is no worry whatsoever on your visit, even if you don't speak a word of Japanese.
- *Top Tips for Visiting Disneyland Paris*. A guide to arriving in Paris and making your way to the theme park, as well as in-depth information about what to expect when you arrive, and how you can best plan.
- *Magic Quizdom*: A trivia book dedicated only to Disneyland, this book specializes in historical items and dates for Walt's original Magic Kingdom.
- *101 Things You Never Knew About Disneyland*. Hidden history and insider tributes abound at Disneyland, and this book charts all of them, to make your visit to Disneyland all the more magical by reveling in the history all around you.
- *Jason's Disneyland Almanac*. A daily history of Disneyland from 1955-2010, with every significant event chronicled and indexed.

These works can be ordered from online bookseller Amazon.com and several are available as electronic Kindle books.

An online blogger and columnist since 1997, Kevin now publishes primarily at UltimateOrlando.com.

Index

100 Years of Magic	104
1901	13, 14
1923	81
1928	79
1952	79
1955	30, 53, 54, 55, 83
1964 World's Fair	25, 113
1971	11, 12, 30, 35, 39, 49, 88, 92, 93
1982	30, 64
1989	30, 101
1998	30, 112, 114
20,000 Leagues Under the Sea	27, 31, 32, 34, 124
A113	96
ABC Sound Studio	124
ACME	98, 102
Admiral Joe Fowler (steamboat)	44, 45
Adventure Thru Inner Space	92, 95
Adventurers Club	52, 100, 120
Affection Section	110
Africa Pavilion	72
Ali San San	94
Alien Encounter	22, 120, 124
Allen, Bob	127
America Sings	50, 91
America the Beautiful	24, 124
American Adventure	72, 73, 74, 123
American Idol Experience	82, 123
American Journeys	124
Anaheim Produce	77
Anderson, Ken	83, 104
Annakin, Kenneth	54
Apple Dumpling Gang	50
Armstrong, Jim	126
Astro Orbiter	22, 122
Atencio, Xavier	39, 71, 127
Aunt Polly's	47
Aurebesh	95
Ayefour Corporation	20
Baby Herman's Runaway Baby Buggy Ride	99
Backlot Express	95, 99
Backlot Tour	82, 100, 101, 123
Backstage Magic with Mickey Mouse	14, 15
Backstage Pass	102, 124
Bagnall, Michael	126
Baker, Buddy	126
Ballew, Chuck	24
Bambi	92
Barnstormer at Goofy's Wiseacre Farm	31, 122
Barrett, Steve	121
Baxter, Tony	43, 48, 49, 90, 126
Be Our Guest	33
Beastlie Kingdomme	107, 108
Beauty and the Beast – Live on Stage	123
Benny the Cab	99
Bertino, Al	48, 127
Best Friends Pet Care	56
Beumer, Ron	86
Beyer, Steve	81
Big Red	109
Big Thunder Mountain Railroad	48, 65, 122
Bigeaut, Bob	127
Bistro de Paris	75
Black Hole	92
Blair, Mary	38, 105, 118, 127
Boag, Wally	84
Bocuse, Paul	75
Boneyard	113
Bongirno, Carl	127
Booth, Bob	126
Bosche, Bill	127
Bowman, Ron	127
Boxley, David	75
Boyd, Jack	127
Bradbury, Ray	58
Brennan, Patrick	83
Bright, Randy	73
Broggie, Roger	126
Broggie, Roger Jr.	126
Brown Derby	80
Browning, Nolan	127
Brummitt, Howard	127
Bruns, George	126
Bullard, Ed	126
Burke, Jeff	73
Burke, Pat	48
Burkhart, Dave	39, 126
Burley, Fred	84
Burley, Fulton	62
Burns, Harriet	42, 72
Buzz Lightyear's Space Ranger Spin	23, 24, 122
Bwana Bob's	55
C3PO	87
Campbell, Collin	127
Captain EO	92, 123
Carlson, Joyce	17, 19, 38, 105, 126
Carolwood Pacific Railroad	12, 31, 117
Carousel of Progress	21, 25, 42, 57, 122
Carthay Circle Theater	77, 78
Casablanca	81, 87
Casey's Corner	21
Casting Agency	12
Cayne, Doug	127
Celebrate a Dream Come True	55
Chakranadi Chicken Shop	111

Chapman, Ken	127
Chester and Hester	112
Chicken Little	82
Chisholm, Ed	127
Cinderella Castle	35, 36, 120
Cinderella's Golden Carrousel	124
Cinderella's Royal Table	35
Circle of Life	123
Circle-Vision	24
Clark, Pete	127
Coats, Claude	39, 126
Cobb, Malcom	127
Cockerell, Lee	127
Colonel's Cotton Mill	120
CommuniCore	124
Conservation Station	124
Corson, Charles	126
Cosmic Ray's Starlight Café	28, 71
Countdown to Extinction	114, 124
Country Bear Christmas Special	124
Country Bear Jamboree	48, 122
Country Bear Vacation Hoedown	124
Cover Story	76
Creekmore, Ken	127
Crimmings, Pete	127
Crockett, Davy	45
Crowell, Ted	126
Crump, Rolly	38, 40, 41, 106
Crystal Arts	19
Curry, John	126
Dains, Hank	127
Dancing Man	104
Dapper Dans	12
Dare, Bud	127
DASA	92
David-Hoffman, Agnes	19
Davis, Marc	39, 43, 48, 51, 83, 126
Davis, Marvin	127
Davy Crockett Explorer Canoes	45, 124
DeCuir, John	126
Diamond Horseshoe Jamboree	124
Diamond Horseshoe Revue	124
Diamond Horseshoe Saloon Revue	124
Dick Tracy Diamond Double-Cross	101, 124
Dingman, Dan	127
Dino-Rama	112
Dinosaur	112, 114, 115, 123
Dinosaur Jubilee	115, 124
Dip Site #1138	81
Discovery Island	117, 124
Discovery River Boat Tour	107
Discovery River Taxis	107
Disney Afternoon	84
Disney Cruise Line	16
Disney Junior – Live on Stage	123
Disney Vacation Club	113
Disney, Abigail	127
Disney, Elias	14, 127
Disney, Kepple	44
Disney, Patty	127
Disney, Roy E.	20, 127
Disney, Roy O.	11, 20, 127
Disney, Roy Patrick	127
Disney, Susan	127
Disney, Timothy	127
Disney, Walt	10, 13, 14, 20, 35, 44, 46, 96, 104, 127
Disney's DOUG Live!	82, 124
Disneylandia	104
Disney-MGM Studios	77, 100
DisneyQuest	120
Docter, Pete	102
Donald's Boat	124
Dream Suite	36
Dream Vehicle	67, 69, 106
Dreamfinder	66, 67
Dreamflight	24, 124
Dumbo the Flying Elephant	122
Durflinger, Glenn	127
Dyer, Bonar	127
Earth Day	114
Eastman, Tom	127
Echo Lake	99
Echo Lake Apartments	81
Edgren, Don	126
Eisner, Michael	66
El Pirata y el Perico	51
El Rio Del Tiempo	71, 124
Elephant Tales	52
Ellen's Energy Adventure	58, 123
Enchanted Tales with Belle	122
Enchanted Tiki Room	122
Enchanted Tiki Room Under New Management	124
EPCOT Center	64, 70
Esselstrom, Doug	86
Evans, Bill	83, 127
Evans, Dick	127
Expedition Everest	123
Experimental Prototype Community of Tomorrow	21
Fagrell, Norm	127
Fantasmic!	123
Father of the Bride	117
FedEx	28, 88
Ferges, Jack	127
Ferrante, Orlando	20, 127
Festival of the Lion King	123
Figment	66, 67
Figment's Place	68
Finding Nemo	123
Firehouse Five Plus Two	30
Fitzgerald, Tom	67, 91
Fleischer, Charles	88
Flight to the Moon	22, 124
Flights of Wonder	123
Florida Citrus Growers	52

Food Rocks	124
Fort Collins	53
Fort Langhorn	46
Fort Langhorn Cantina	47
Fort Sam Clemens	46
Fort Wilderness Railroad	118
Foster, Bob	127
Fowler, Chuck	127
Fowler, Joe	10
Frank, Laurence	109
Frankie, John	126
Frontierland Shootin' Arcade	46, 122
Fulton's Crab House	62
Fulton's General Store	62
Gallagher, Neil	126
Garves, Stan	126
General Electric	25
General Joe Potter (steamboat)	44
Gengenbach, Dave	126
Gertie the Dinosaur	80
Get Happy with ABC	82, 124
Ghost Host	41
Gibson, Blaine	48, 73, 106, 127
Gillett, Jack	86
Gladish, Jack	126
Glendale	25, 26, 80, 85, 90
Goff, Harper	31, 40, 46, 53, 83, 104
Golden Dreams	76
Golden Oak Outpost	50
Goodall, Jane	108
Goosebumps HorrorLand Fright Show and FunHouse	101
Gorilla Falls	109
Gracey, Yale	38, 39, 127
Gran Fiesta Tour	71, 123
Grand Prix Raceway	29
Grandt, Jason	16, 69
Granny's Cabin	104
Gray, Judi	42
Great Moments with Mr. Lincoln	41, 106
Great Movie Ride	86, 87, 123
Greathouse, Cicero	19
Green, Vic	127
Greenberg, Adrian	76
Griffith, Doug	86
Gurr, Bob	126
Hall of Presidents	43, 56, 106, 122
Hall, Clem	48
Harrison Hightower IV	84
Harryman, Orpha	127
Hartley, Paul	127
Haunted Mansion	39, 41, 42, 43, 106, 122
Head, Edith	76
Headless Horseman	43
Heffron, Jim	19
Hench, John	27, 43, 127
Henning, Doug	52
Henson, Jim	97
Here Come the Muppets	85, 98, 124
Hibler, Winston	53
Holloway, Sterling	96
Holly Vermont Realty	81
Holmby Hills	11
Holmes, Phil	33
Holmquist, Don	127
Honey I Shrunk the Audience	124
Honey I Shrunk the Kids Movie Set Adventure	123
Hope, Bob	55
Hope, Fred	127
Horizons	28, 59, 68, 95, 106, 124
Houser, Morrie	126
Hudson River Valley	43
Huet, Cliff	39
Hunchback of Notre Dame: A Musical Adventure	124
Hutchinson, Helena	48
Hyperion	27
If You Could Fly	124
If You Had Wings	24, 71, 124
Illusioneering	17, 73
ImageWorks	123
Impressions de France	74, 123
Indiana Jones Epic Stunt Spectacular	88, 123
Innoventions	123
Irvine, Richard	127
Irving, Washington	43
It's a Small World	38, 122
It's a Wonderful Life	81
It's Tough to be a Bug	108, 124
Iwerks, Don	127
Iwerks, Ub	127
Jackman, Bob	126
Jackson, Michael	46
Jackson, Wilfred	15
Jacobson, Eric	86
Jani, Robert	126
Janney, Alison	94
Jar Jar Binks	92, 93
Jedi Training Academy	123
Jefferds, Vince	127
Jennings, Lou	126
Joelscher, Bill	127
Joerger, Fred	39, 42, 48, 127
Johnson, Ed	126
Johnston, Ollie	83, 84
Jolley, Stan	48
Joslin, Bob	86
Journey into Imagination	15, 66, 124
Journey Into Imagination With Figment	123
Journey into Jungle Book	124
Journey into Narnia	124
Journey into Your Imagination	124
Joyce, John	126
Jue, Daniel	111
Jungle Cruise	52, 53, 54, 87, 122
Justice, Bill	15, 126

Kali River Rapids	124
K-DROID	93
Keehne, John	127
Kent, Ralph	126
Kilimanjaro Safari	109, 124
Kim Possible World Showcase Adventure	51
Kimball, Ward	12, 15, 30, 83
Kirk, Tim	86
Kitchen Kabaret	64, 106, 125
Kline, Dick	127
Klug, Ken	126
Koch, Glenn	86
Kodak	68
Kramer, Joe	127
Kuri, Emile	126
La Signature	75
Lange, Skip	48
LaNotre, Gaston	75
LaPere, Richard	37
Lasseter, John	82, 83, 104
Laugh-O-Grams	80
Laval, Bruce	127
Le Chapeau	18
Lee, Katherine	94
Legend of the Lion King	37, 125
Liberty Belle	44, 122
Lights Motors Action	123
Lights of Winter	70
Lindberg, Arnold	126
Lindley, Lonnie	126
Lindquist, Jack	126
Listen to the Land	125
Living Easels	120
Living Seas	62, 80, 125
Living with the Land	65, 123
Logan, Ron	126
Looney Bin	102
Lucas, George	89
Lund, Bradford	127
Lund, Michelle	127
Lund, Victoria	127
Lund, William	127
Luxo Ball	30
Luxo Jr	103
MacArthur, James	54
Mad Tea Party	122
Madame Leota	18, 92
Maelstrom	123
Magic Carpet 'Round the World	24, 125
Magic Carpets of Aladdin	122
Magic Journeys	37, 68, 125
Magic of Disney Animation	82, 83, 123
Main Street Cinema	19, 125
Main Street Vehicles	122
Many Adventures of Winnie the Pooh	34, 122
Market House	19
Markham, Pete	127
Martin, Bill	39, 127
Martin, Bud	127
Mary Poppins	75
Maslak, Stan	126
Matheison, Bob	127
McCarthy, Bob	73
McCay, Windsor	80
McClure, Neal	127
McCrumb, Thomas	14
McDonald's	114
McGinnis, George	126
McGuire, Dorothy	54
McKim, Brian	72
McKim, Sam	72, 127
McLean, Marianne	95
McManus, Jim	127
Mdundo Kibanda	72
Meet the World	74
Merchant of Venus	23
Mesa Verde	28
Mickey Mouse One	101
Mickey Mouse Revue	27, 37, 125
Mickey's Birthdayland	125
Mickey's Country House	125
Mickey's Hollywood Theater	125
Mickey's Philharmagic	37, 122
Mickey's Starland	125
Mickey's Toontown Fair	18, 33
Midler, Bette	100
Mighty Ducks of Anaheim	102, 119
Mike Fink Keel Boats	45, 118, 125
Mile Long Bar	50
Miller, Christopher	127
Miller, Jennifer	127
Miller, Joanna	127
Miller, Patrick	127
Miller, Ron	127
Miller, Ronald Jr.	127
Miller, Tamara	127
Miller, Walter	127
Millington, Frank	127
Mills, John	54
Min and Bill	81
Mine Train Through Nature's Wonderland	48
Mineral Springs Ski Resort	48
Minnie's Country House	125
Miss Liberty	36
Mission Space	59, 60
Mission to Mars	22, 27, 60, 88, 125
Mittermeier, Russell	111
Mlle. Lafayette's Parfumerie	44
Mogul Mania	116
Moline, Robert	58
Monster Sound Show	125
Monsters, Inc. Laugh Floor	24, 122
Moore, Fred	15
Moore, Robert	127

Morrow, Dick	127
Morrow, Tom	22
Mortimer Mouse	79, 85
Mouse Gear	69
Mr. Johnson	22, 60
Mr. Toad's Wild Ride	16, 27, 34, 41, 96, 125
Mulholland, Jenny	94
Multiplane Camera	46, 59
MuppetVision 3-D	97, 123
Museum of the Weird	41
Myall, Chuck	39, 127
Nabbe, Tom	127
Nahtezu	109
Natsume, Mitz	127
Nautilus	34
NBC Pipes	97
Nelson, George	127
Newton, Ernie	84
Nine Old Men	83
Noceti, Norm	127
Nunis, Dick	127
O Canada	123
O'Brien, Ken	127
Oasis	54
Oasis Canteen	81
Old World Antiques	44
Olin, Spence	127
Olsen, Jack	127
Olson, Jeff	73
Olson, John	81
Once Upon a Time	77
One Little Spark	67
One Man's Dream	123
Orange Bird	52, 84
Osborne, Jennings	97
Osterhaut, Paul	86
Oswald the Lucky Rabbit	16, 85
Oz, Frank	97
Pan Galactic Pizza Port	28
Pangani Forest	109
Parris, Diego	77
Paskevicius, Alyja	127
Passilla, James	127
Pausch, Randy	33
Peet, Bill	96
Peevy's Polar Pipeline	81
Peirce, Tom	127
Pena, Rudy	126
PeopleMover	21, 22, 24, 122
Pepper's Ghost	115
Perry, Joe	79
Peter Pan's Flight	122
Pfahler, Dick	127
Pharaoh Mickey	86
Phelps, Bob	127
Pirates of the Caribbean	51, 106, 122
Playhouse Disney Live	125
Plaza Swan Boats	21, 27, 125
Pleasure Island	52
Plummer, Elmer	127
Polynesian Resort	116
Pope, Owen	126
Popham, Osh	18
Port Orleans Riverside	120
Potter, Joe	10, 13, 44, 127
Primeval Whirl	124
Prince Charming Regal Carrousel	36, 122
Prinzhorn, Ernie	127
Progress City	21
Project Little Man	53
Puckett, Geoff	86
Quest of the Unicorn	107
R2-D2	87
R2-MK	93
Radio Disney	88
Radio Disney River Cruise	107
Rafiki's Planet Watch	124
Raiders of the Lost Ark	81
Rainbow Caverns	49
Ranft, Joe	103
Ravenscroft, Thurl	39, 42, 84
RCA	28
Reardon, Robin	86
Redmond, Dorothea	35, 127
Reflections of China	123
Reifsnyder, Frank	95
Reiser, Larry	127
Renault	74
Restaurantosaurus	112, 113, 114
Rex	90, 92
Rhine River Cruise	71
Richard F. Irvine (steamboat)	44
Ridgway, Charlie	126
River Country	117, 125
Rivera, Jonas	102
Robertson, Warren	127
Robinson, Cecil	126
Rock 'n' Roller Coaster	79, 80, 123
Rocketeer	99
Rogers, Kathy	86
Rogers, Wathel	39, 53, 127
Rogers, Will	74
Rohde, Joe	52, 110, 111, 113
Roland, Howard	126
Roser, Katie	19
Rosie's All-American Café	78
Rosita	49
Ross, Jim	127
Rothschild, Rick	72
Rotundo, Carol	86
Russell, Craig	86
Russell, Kurt	67
Ryman, Herb	26, 43, 127
Sayers, Jack	127

Scharff, Hanns	35	*Swapp, Eric*	86
Schweninger, Dave	126	*Swiss Family Treehouse*	54, 122
Sci-Fi Dine-In Restaurant	80, 88	*Sword in the Stone*	36
Seabase Alpha	62, 63	*Symbiosis*	64, 125
Seven Dwarfs Mine Train	122	*Take Flight*	24, 125
Sewell, Bob	39, 127	*Tarzan*	87
Sewelson, Cory	86	*Tarzan Rocks*	125
Short, Martin	117	*Tatum, Donn*	127
Show Biz Is.	125	*Test Track*	123
Sights & Sounds	76	*Texas John Slaughter*	47
Silversmith	44	*The Computer Wore Tennis Shoes*	67
Sinkhole	70	*The Lottery*	100
Sklar, Marty	26, 67, 127	*The Producers*	81
Skyppy	23	*The Seas With Nemo and Friends*	62, 63, 123
Skyway	125	*Thoman, Brock*	86
Skyway to Fantasyland	27	*Thomas, Frank*	83, 84
Sleepy Hollow Refreshments	43	*THX1138*	81
Slocum, Larry	127	*Ticket Books*	11
Smelser, Marshall	127	*Ticket Booth*	29
Smith, Phil	127	*Tiger Rapids Run*	112
Snow White and the Seven Dwarfs	77, 78	*Tilley, Scott*	15
Snow White's Scary Adventures	32, 37, 125	*Timekeeper*	24, 125
Snyder, David	126	*TK421*	90
Soarin'	123	*Tobacconist Shop*	19
Soarin' Over California	65	*Tom Sawyer Island*	122
Sorcerer Mickey	26	*Tomorrowland Grand Prix Raceway*	125
Sounds Dangerous	125	*Tomorrowland Indy Speedway*	29
Space Mountain	27, 88, 122	*Tomorrowland Speedway*	122
Space Station X-1	28	*Tonarely, Lou*	127
Spaceship Earth	56, 57, 58, 123	*Toombs, Leota*	38, 39
Spartacus	53	*Toontown Trolley*	99
SpectroMagic	55	*Tower of Terror*	79, 123
Spiegel, Steven	95	*Tower of the Four Winds*	106
Spirit of Pocahontas	125	*Toy Story Midway Mania*	103, 123
Splash	99	*Toy Story Parade*	98
Splash Mountain	122	*Trader Sam*	83
Sprout, Michael	86	*Transportation and Ticket Center*	10
Stage 1 Company Store	98	*Treasure Island*	125
Stanek, Francis	127	*Treasure of the Incas*	119
Star Jets	22, 125	*Tree of Life*	108
Star of the Day	98	*TriceraTop Spin*	124
Star Tours	123	*TRON*	92
Starring Rolls Café	80	*Tropical Serenade*	52, 84, 125
Steel, Walt	86	*Tryon, Larry*	127
Steward, McLaren	127	*Turtle Talk with Crush*	63, 123
Stitch's Great Escape	22, 122	*Twain, Mark*	46
STOLport	96, 101	*Universe of Energy*	58, 59, 125
Streets of America	96	*Vale, Mike*	86
Strode, Woody	53	*Van Every, Dick*	126
Sullivan, Bill	127	*Vaughn, Pat*	127
Sullivan, John	86	*Verge, Roger*	75
Summer Magic	18	*Verity, Jim*	126
Summers, Dan	97	*Viking Ship*	71
Sunset Blvd	78	*Vilmer, Earl*	13, 126
Sunshine Tree Terrace	52	*Virginia, Tony*	127
Superstar Television	82, 125	*Voyage of the Little Mermaid*	123
Surrell, Jason	39, 50	*Walker, Card*	126

Wall-E	92
Walsh, Bill	126
Walt Disney Imagineering	15, 25, 57, 62, 80, 96, 114
Walt Disney Story	125
Walt Disney World Railroad	11, 45, 122
Warburton, Patrick	65, 93
Washo, Bill	127
Washo, Bud	127
Watkins, Bill	126
Watt, Wilbur	127
Wave Machine	116
WEDway PeopleMover	125
Weis, Bob	86
Wells, Frank	110, 127
Western River Expedition	49, 65
Who Wants to be a Millionaire-Play it!	125
Wilderness Lodge	117
William Morris Agency	85
Williams, Gordon	39, 127
Wilson's Cave Inn	45
Windrum, George	127
Wise, John	126
Wizard of Oz	87
Wonders of China	125
Wonders of Life	10, 125
World of Motion	61, 100, 125
WorldKey	58
Wyss, Johann David	54
X-S Tech	23, 25, 120
Yak and Yeti	111
Ye Olde Christmas Shoppe	44
Younger, Gary	126
Zovich, John	126

Printed in Great Britain
by Amazon